NCAA RECRUIT TIPS:
7 STEPS TO A SCHOLARSHIP
2017 EDITION

WRITTEN BY: @1001RECRUITTIPS
               A.P. BAH BIOH

@1001RecruitTips

No part of this publication may be reproduced, stored in a retrieval system or transmitted in any form or by any means, electronic, mechanical, photocopying, recording, scanning or otherwise.

This publication is an independent information source not approved, recommended, associated with or prepared by the NCAA, NAIA or any individual coach or university.

Trademarks: NCAA is a trademark or registered trademark of The National Collegiate Athletic Association. All trademarks are the property of their respective owners.

LIMIT OF LIABILITY/DISCLAIMER OF WARRANTY: The publisher and the author make no representations or warranties with respect to the accuracy or completeness of the contents of this work and specifically disclaim all warranties, including without limitation warranties of fitness for a particular purpose. No warranty may be created or extended by sales or promotional materials, the advice and strategies contained herein may not be suitable for every situation. This work is sold with the understanding that the publisher is not engaged in rendering legal, accounting, or other professional services. If professional assistance is required, the services of a competent professional person should be sought, neither the publisher nor the author shall be liable for damages arising herefrom, the fact that an organization or website is referred to in this work as a citation and/or a potential source of further information does not mean that the author or the publisher endorses the information the organization or website may provide or recommendations it may make, further, readers should be aware that internet websites listed in this work may have changed or disappeared between when this work was written and when it is read

Text Copyright © 2016 All Rights Reserved

All rights reserved. ISBN: 0-9859048-7-9
ISBN-13: 978-0-9859048-7-6

NCAA RECRUIT TIPS: 7 STEPS TO A SCHOLARSHIP

TO MY AMAZING DAUGHTER...
(FUTURE SOCCER SIGNING CLASS OF 2031)

EVERY DAY YOU MAKE US SMILE AND LAUGH, AND TEACH US SOMETHING NEW. I HOPE YOU KNOW, EVERY DAY, HOW MUCH WE LOVE YOU!

AND TO ALL THOSE DEDICATED STUDENT-ATHLETES OUT THERE – I HOPE THIS BOOK WILL HELP YOU ACHIEVE ALL OF YOUR GOALS AND DREAMS!

PLEASE TAKE A MOMENT TO REVIEW THIS BOOK ON AMAZON, TO HELP OTHER STUDENT-ATHLETES AND THEIR FAMILIES FIND SUCCESS IN THE PROCESS!

@1001RecruitTips

TABLE OF CONTENTS

STEP #1 – UNDERSTANDING MANDATORY REQUIREMENTS

Upcoming NLI Signing Dates - NCAA......10
What is the Difference Between NCAA & NAIA......10
What is an NLI: National Letter of Intent......11
What Do NCAA Athletic Scholarships Cover......11
Registering with the NCAA Eligibility Center......11
What You Need to Know About the NCAA Eligibility Center......11
ACT/SAT Upcoming Test Dates......12
Athletic Scholarships: Are they 4-Year or Year-to-Year?......13
Academics: Each University Sets Own Standards......13
NCAA Division I Academic Standards......14
NCAA Division II Academic Standards......16
NCAA Division III Academic Standards......18
NAIA Academic Standards......18
Students with Documented Education-Impacting Disabilities......19
Academic Documentation for Home School Students......21
NCAA Recruiting Definitions......22
Action Steps: Mandatory Requirements......24

STEP #2 - GETTING STARTED & GETTING NOTICED

Scholarship Offers: Earned, Not Given......26
Odds of Playing After High School......28
#1 Rule to Get Noticed......28
The First Question Coaches Will Ask You......28
Putting Together Your Student-Athlete Resume......29
Don't Pay Services to Get Your Name Out to Recruiters......31
Start Local......31
There is a Method to the Madness......33
8 Reasons Why Players Begin to Get Recruited......34
8 Reasons: Scouting Services......35
8 Reasons: Combines......37
8 Reasons: Games and Tournaments......39
8 Reasons: Recommended by Coach......42
8 Reasons: Camps......45
10 Tips to Go From Camper to Recruit......46
8 Reasons: Highlight video......49
15 Tips For Putting Together Your Highlight Video......50
Highlights vs. Game Video......51
How to Get the Coach's Contact Info......52
8 Reasons: Were Offered By a Rival or Comparable School......56
8 Reasons: Political Ties......56
Interest vs. Scholarship Offers......58
Getting the First Scholarship Offer......58
Action Steps: Getting Started & Getting Noticed......60

STEP #3 - UNDERSTANDING HOW COACHES EVALUATE PLAYERS & BUILD SIGNING CLASS

How Coaches Assign Recruiting Responsibilities...62
How the Coaching Staff Ranks Players...64
How Coaches Build Their "Watch Lists"..65
What's More Important - Size vs. Skill...66
Will Leading the League in Stats Help Me Get Noticed?......................................67
One Sport vs. Dual Sport Players...68
Can You Qualify Academically...69
No Stone Unturned..70
From Building Watch Lists to First Day of Class...72
Tell Me More About Yourself - Answering Interview-Style Questions................73
How to Carry Yourself When Approaching Coaches..74
Questions About Playing Time..75
Keeping Your Recruiting Coaches Updated on Who Has Offered You..............76
What to Expect: Freshman Year of HS..77
What to Expect: Sophomore Year of HS...78
What to Expect: Junior Year of HS..80
What to Expect: Senior Year of HS..84
When College Coaches Can Contact: By Sport..88
Before the Scholarship Offer: 20 Signs a Coach is Interested............................99
Your Decision Timeline..100
The Woo-ing Stage..101
Closing the Deal on Home Turf..101
Pressure Time to Commit...102
14 Signs of a Great Recruiter..104
Action Steps: Understanding How Coaches Build Their Signing Classes..........106

STEP #4 - DEVELOPING AND NARROWING YOUR LIST

Develop Your List: What's Important to You...110
30 Factors Recruits Consider When Selecting a School....................................110
20 Signs of a Successful College Coach..112
Questions to Ask During the Recruiting Process..113
10 Must-Ask Questions During Recruiting Process and Campus Visits..........114
More Potential Questions to Ask..115
What to Expect on Unofficial/Official Visits...119
Setting Up a Visit to a School That Has Not Shown Interest Yet.....................121
Keep Detailed Notes: Write Thoughts Down in the Moment............................122
Full Scholarships vs. Partial Scholarships...122
The Money Talk: Asking What Scholarship Offer Will Cover............................124
After Offer, How Long Do Coaches Hold Scholarship for You?........................125
Can Coaches Pull Scholarship After You've Verbally Committed?...................125
What You Need to Know About Committing..126
Action Steps: Developing & Narrowing Your List..127

STEP #5 - HOW TO HELP YOUR CAUSE
Coaches Are Evaluating Everything About You..130
What Makes You Unique...130
Timing is Everything...131
8 Tips to Help You Gain Weight..132
25 Tips to Become a Better Leader...132
10 Sacrifices You Can Make to Become a Better Player.................................135
14 Ways to Improve Time Management..135
Direct Line of Communication...138
Respond to Questionnaires..138
Social Media & Recruiting: 16 Tips Before You Post...139
Don't Become a Pest...141
Action Steps: How to Help Your Cause...142

STEP #6 - IF PLAN 'A' ISN'T WORKING OUT...
When You Don't Feel Like You're Improving Athletically..................................146
How to Improve Mental Toughness...147
How to Repair Character Issues...148
Not Hearing Anything Back from Coaches After Sending Video....................149
I've Started Several Games and Got Benched, Should I Transfer?...............150
Will Suspensions End My Recruitment?...151
What if There is a Chance in Coaches?..152
15 Tips for Adjusting to a New Coach...154
The Right to Change Your Mind..155
10 Tips for Unsigned Seniors...156
The Junior College Route...157
Walk-On Opportunities...158
30 Tips for Walk-Ons: How to Make the Team and Earn Playing Time........159
Do Walk-Ons Ever Earn Scholarship Money?...164
How to Pay for School Outside of Athletic Scholarships.................................165
Dealing with Issues with the NCAA...166
Plan to Transfer in a Year or Two to Jump to Higher Division........................166
What if an Injury Interrupts my Career...167
Ways to Address Issues with Your Child's Coach..168
Action Steps: If Plan 'A' Isn't Working Out..170

STEP #7 - REMAIN IN CONTROL
Never Put an Expiration Date on Your Dreams...174
Always Remain in Control..174
Signed, Sealed & Delivered: Advice for Scholarship Signees..........................175
14 Tips for Your First Month on Campus..177
Action Steps: Remain in Control...180

@1001RecruitTips

STEP #1
UNDERSTANDING MANDATORY REQUIREMENTS

"Concentrate on one goal. Nobody ever reached their potential by scattering themselves in 20 directions. Reaching your potential requires focus."
-JOHN C. MAXWELL

"There's a difference in interest and commitment. When interested, you do something when convenient. When committed you accept no excuses."
-KEN BLANCHARD

"Success is the sum of small efforts repeated day in and day out."
-ROBERT COLLIER

UPCOMING SIGNING DATES: 2017-18 ENROLLMENT

Basketball
Early Period -   November 9, 2016-November 16, 2016
Regular Period -   Division I - April 12, 2017 - May 17, 2017
                   Division II - April 12, 2017 - August 1, 2017

Football
Midyear JC Transfer - December 14, 2016 - January 15, 2017
Regular Period -   February 1, 2017 - April 1, 2017

Soccer and Men's Water Polo
February 1, 2017 -   August 1, 2017

All Other Sports
Early Period -   November 9, 2016 - November 16, 2016
Regular Period -   April 12, 2017 - August 1, 2017

WHAT IS THE DIFFERENCE: NCAA VS. NAIA?

NCAA: The NCAA (National Collegiate Athletic Association) is made up of three divisions (I, II and III) and is made up of nearly 1,100 member colleges and universities that provide more than $2.7 billion dollars worth of scholarship money. Over 480,000 athletes participate in NCAA athletics with over 150,000 receiving athletic scholarship aid. Competition at Division I is considered the highest level, and athletes within Division I and II eligible to earn scholarship money. Division III institutions do NOT offer athletic aid, but student-athletes may receive academic or other need-based aid to assist with tuition. For more information, visit ncaa.org to learn about each division.

NAIA: The NAIA (National Association of Intercollegiate Athletics) is an organization that is made up of over 250 member colleges and universities that sponsors national championships in 23 different intercollegiate sports. Overall, the member institutions provide over $500 million dollars in scholarship aid to over 65,000 student-athletes across the country. For more information, visit NAIA.org.

OVER $500 MILLION IN SCHOLARSHIP MONEY AT OVER 250 NAIA INSTITUTIONS

The level of competition is considered higher among NCAA institutions (going in order from toughest: Division I to Division II to Division III), but the NAIA provides great opportunities for high school athletes looking to continue playing at the collegiate level—while sometimes earning scholarship money too.

NLI: NCAA NATIONAL LETTERS OF INTENT
The NLI (National Letter of Intent) is a binding agreement between a prospective student-athlete and an NLI member institution.

    - Prospective student-athlete agrees to attend the institution full-time for one academic year (two semesters or three quarters).
    - Institution agrees to provide athletics financial aid for one academic year (two semesters or three quarters).
    - Coaching Change: A prospective student-athlete signs an NLI with an institution. If the coach leaves, the NLI signee is still bound by the provisions of the NLI.

<u>Basic Penalty for not fulfilling the NLI agreement:</u> Serve one year in residence (full-time two semesters or three quarters) at the next NLI member institution and lose one season of competition at next school.

WHAT DO NCAA ATHLETIC SCHOLARSHIPS COVER?
NCAA Division I and II athletics scholarships are awarded in a variety of amounts. Colleges and universities are permitted to provide a student-athlete with tuition and fees, room, board and required course-related books and supplies.

REGISTERING WITH THE NCAA ELIGIBILITY CENTER
There is one mandatory step in order to accept a scholarship from a Division I or Division II institution, registering with the NCAA Eligibility Center and completing certification that verifies your academic requirements and status as an amateur athlete.

WHAT YOU NEED TO KNOW ABOUT THE NCAA ELIGIBILITY CENTER...

- You must register with the NCAA Eligibility Center (www.EligibilityCenter.org) in order to practice, play and receive a Division I or Division II athletic scholarship. You may register at any time, but it is recommend that you begin the process during your sophomore or junior year of high school.

- Academic requirements are not the same between Division I and Division II (and Division III). You may qualify for one division and not qualify for another. It's best to be prepared to qualify for all!

- Academic Requirements:
    #1 - Graduate from high school
    #2 - Complete a minimum number of NCAA-approved core courses (varies by division and graduation year)
    #3 - Earn a minimum GPA in those NCAA-approved core courses
    #4 - Earn a required SAT or ACT sum score, dependent on Division I or II standards.

- Only courses that appear on your school's List of NCAA Courses will be used in the calculation of the core GPA. Be sure to look at your high school's List of NCAA Courses at www.eligibilitycenter.org.

- Your SAT/ACT scores must be reported DIRECTLY from the testing agencies, test scores that appear on transcripts will not be used. When registering for the SAT or ACT, use the NCAA Eligibility Center code of 9999 to ensure that your scores are reported directly to the NCAA.

- The SAT score used for NCAA purposes includes ONLY the critical reading and match sections. (The writing section of SAT is not used.)

- The ACT score used for NCAA purposes is the sum of the following four sections: English, mathematics, reading and science.

ACT/SAT UPCOMING TEST DATES
ACT TEST DATES
Below are dates for upcoming 2017 and beyond ACT Tests. Please note, you must be pre-registered in order to take the test, with the regular registration deadline 5-6 weeks prior to the test. To register or for more information on the ACT Test, visit ACTStudent.org.

Test Dates	Registration Deadline	Late Registration
February 11, 2017*	January 13, 2017	January 14-20, 2017
April 8, 2017	March 3, 2017	March 4-17, 2017
June 10, 2017	May 5, 2017	May 6-19, 2017

Tentative Dates for 2017-18 Academic Year: September 9, 2017; October 28, 2017; December 9, 2017; Feb 10, 2018; April 14, 2018; June 9, 2018.

THE ACT OFFERS A FREE PRACTICE GUIDE AT THEIR WEBSITE, ACTSTUDENT.ORG.

SAT TEST DATES
Below are dates for upcoming 2017 SAT Tests. Please note, you must be pre-registered in order to take the test, with the regular registration deadline one month prior to the test. To register or for more information on the SAT Test, visit SAT.collegeboard.org.

Test Dates	Registration Deadline	Late Registration
January 21, 2017	December 21, 2016	January 10, 2017
March 11, 2017	February 10, 2017	February 28, 2017
May 6, 2017	April 7, 2017	April 25, 2017
June 3, 2017	May 9, 2017	May 24, 2017

Tentative Dates for 2017-19 Academic Years: August 26, 2017; October 7, 2017; November 4, 2017; December 2, 2017; March 10, 2018; May 5,

NCAA RECRUIT TIPS: 7 STEPS TO A SCHOLARSHIP

2018; June 2, 2018; August 25, 2018; October 6, 2018; November 3, 2018; December 1, 2018; March 9, 2019; May 4, 2019; June 1, 2019.

TO TAKE A FREE PRACTICE TEST, VISIT WWW.KHANACADEMY.ORG/SAT.

REPORT SAT/ACT TEST SCORES DIRECTLY TO ELIGIBILITY CENTERS:

NCAA: USE CODE 9999

NAIA: USE CODE 9876

ATHLETIC SCHOLARSHIPS - ARE THEY FOR FOUR YEARS OR YEAR-TO-YEAR?

From the NCAA....At a minimum, an athletics scholarship must be a one academic year agreement. In Division I, colleges and universities are permitted to offer multi-year scholarships. Athletics scholarships may be renewed and the college or university must notify the student-athlete in writing by July 1 whether the athletics scholarship will be renewed for the next academic year. Individual colleges and universities have appeal policies for scholarships that are reduced or not renewed.

ACADEMICS: EACH UNIVERSITY SETS THEIR OWN STANDARDS

It's very important to understand that even though the NCAA Eligibility Center sets their own mandatory minimum requirements for GPAs and test scores, that doesn't guarantee admission to any and every school. Each school sets their own standards and each school varies on the flexibility they grant the Athletic Department in terms of admissions. Don't eliminate your opportunities down the road by only shooting to achieve the minimum academic standards required by the NCAA!

DIVISION I ACADEMIC STANDARDS: FULL QUALIFIER

To be eligible to practice, compete and receive athletics scholarships in your first full-time year at a Division I school, you must graduate high school and meet ALL the following requirements:

#1 - Complete 16 NCAA core courses:
- Four years of English;
- Three years of math (Algebra 1 or higher);
- Two years of natural/physical science (including one year of lab science if your high school offers it);
- Two years of social science;
- One additional year of English, math or natural/physical science; and
- Four additional years of English, math, natural/physical science, social science, foreign language, comparative religion or philosophy.

#2 - Complete 10 core courses, including seven in English, math or natural/physical science, before the start of your seventh semester. Once you begin your seventh semester, you may not repeat or replace any of those 10 courses for GPA improvement.

#3 - Earn at least a 2.3 GPA in your core courses.

#4 - Earn an SAT combined score or ACT sum score that matches your core-course GPA on the Division I Sliding Scale.

WHAT IF I DON'T MEET THE DIVISION I STANDARDS?)...

If you enroll full time at a Division I school, and you have not met all the Division I academic standards, you may not compete in your first year at college. However, if you qualify as an academic redshirt, you may practice during your first term in college and receive an athletics scholarship for the entire year. The academic redshirt qualification is only for students who enroll full time in college.

To qualify as an academic redshirt, you must graduate high school and meet ALL the following academic standards:
1. Complete 16 core courses;
2. Earn at least a 2.0 GPA in your core courses; and 3. Earn an SAT combined score or ACT sum score matching your core-course GPA on the Division I sliding scale.

NCAA RECRUIT TIPS: 7 STEPS TO A SCHOLARSHIP

INITIAL-ELIGIBILITY STANDARDS FOR NCAA DIVISION I

There are four possible initial-eligibility outcomes:

#1 - Qualifier: You may practice, compete and receive athletics scholarships during your first year of enrollment at an NCAA Division I school.

#2 - Academic Redshirt: You may receive an athletics scholarship during your first year of enrollment and may practice during your first regular academic term but may NOT compete during your first year of enrollment. You must pass either eight quarter or nine semester hours in order to practice in the next term.

#3 - Nonqualifier: You will not be able to practice, receive an athletics scholarship or compete during your first year of enrollment at a Division I school.

#4 - Early Academic Qualifier: If you meet specific criteria after six semesters, you may be deemed an early academic qualifier for Division I.

- Minimum SAT combined score (math and critical reading) of 900 OR minimum ACT sum score of 75; and a core-course GPA of 3.000 or higher in a minimum of 14 core courses (below) plus a final high school transcript submitted to the NCAA Eligibility Center after high school graduation:
  1. Three years of English;
  2. Two years of math;
  3. Two years of science;
  4. Two additional years of English, math or science; and
  5. Five additional core courses in any area.

NCAA SLIDING SCALE DIVISION I - PARTIAL LIST
(SEE NCAA.ORG FOR FULL LISTING OF SLIDING SCALE)

Division I: Full Qualifier –
Min 2.300 GPA
ELIGIBLE FOR FINANCIAL AID, PRACTICE AND COMPETITION
CORE GPA / SAT / ACT
3.550 and up / 400 / 37
3.000 / 620 / 52
2.750 / 720 / 59
2.500 / 820 / 68
2.300 / 900 / 75

Division I: Academic Redshirt – Below 2.300 GPA
ELIGIBLE FOR FINANCIAL AID AND PRACTICE ONLY (NOT ELIGIBLE FOR COMPETITION)

CORE GPA / SAT / ACT
2.299 / 910 / 76
2.200 / 940 / 79
2.100 / 980 / 83
2.000 / 1020 / 86

See NCAA.org for the full Division I Sliding Scale, this is only a partial list

DIVISION II STANDARDS

Division II schools require college-bound student-athletes to meet academic standards for NCAA core courses, core course grade-point average (GPA) and test scores. The standards are changing for students who enroll full time for the first time at a Division II school on or after August 1, 2018.

DIVISION II ACADEMIC STANDARDS: If You Enroll BEFORE August 1, 2018

To be eligible to practice, compete and receive an athletics scholarship in your first full-time year at a Division II school, you must graduate high school and meet ALL the following requirements:

#1 Complete 16 core courses:
- Three years of English;
- Two years of math (Algebra 1 or higher);
- Two years of natural or physical science (including one year of lab science if your high school offers it);
- Two years of social science;
- Three additional years of English, math or natural or physical science; and
- Four additional years of English, math, natural or physical science, social science, foreign language, comparative religion or philosophy.

#2 Earn at least a 2.0 GPA in your core courses.

#3 Earn an SAT combined score of 820 or an ACT sum score of 68.

WHAT IF I DON'T MEET THE DIVISION II STANDARDS?
If You Enroll BEFORE August 1, 2018...
If you enroll full time at a Division II school before August 1, 2018, and you have not met all the Division II academic standards, you may not compete in your first year. However, if you meet the standards to be a partial qualifier, you may practice and receive an athletics scholarship in your first year at college. To be a partial qualifier, you must graduate high school and meet ONE of the following standards:
1. Earn a 2.0 GPA in 16 core courses; or
2. Earn an SAT combined score of 820 or an ACT sum score of 68.

NCAA RECRUIT TIPS: 7 STEPS TO A SCHOLARSHIP

DIVISION II ACADEMIC STANDARDS: If You Enroll AFTER August 1, 2018...

To be eligible to practice, compete and receive an athletics scholarship in your first full-time year at a Division II school, you must graduate high school and meet ALL the following requirements:

#1 Complete 16 core courses:
- Three years of English;
- Two years of math (Algebra 1 or higher);
- Two years of natural or physical science (including one year of lab science if your high school offers it);
- Two years of social science;
- Three additional years of English, math or natural or physical science; and
- Four additional years of English, math, natural or physical science, social science, foreign language, comparative religion or philosophy.

#2 Earn at least a 2.2 GPA in your core courses.

#3 Earn an SAT combined score or ACT sum score that matches your core-course GPA on the Division II competition sliding scale.

NCAA SLIDING SCALE DIVISION II- PARTIAL LIST
(SEE NCAA.ORG FOR FULL LISTING OF SLIDING SCALE)

Division II beginning August 1, 2018... To participate in COMPETITION.
CORE GPA/ SAT / ACT
3.300 and up / 400 / 37
3.000 / 520 / 46
2.500 / 720 / 59
2.200 / 840 & up / 70 & up

Division II beginning August 1, 2018... Partial Qualifier (receive aid, practice but not eligible to compete.)
CORE GPA/ SAT / ACT
3.000 and up / 420 / 39
2.500 / 620 / 52
2.200 / 740 / 61
2.000 / 820 & up / 68 & up

WHAT IF I DON'T MEET THE DIVISION II STANDARDS?
If You Enroll AFTER August 1, 2018...
If you enroll full time at a Division II school after August 1, 2018, and you have not met all the Division II academic standards, you may not compete in your first year. However, if you meet the standards to be a partial qualifier, you may practice and receive an athletics scholarship in your first year at college. To be a partial qualifier, you must graduate high school and meet ALL the following standards:
1. Complete 16 core courses;
2. Earn at least a 2.0 GPA in your core courses; and
3. Earn an SAT combined score or ACT sum score matching your core-course GPA on the Division II partial qualifier sliding scale.

DIVISION III ACADEMIC STANDARDS:
ATHLETIC SCHOLARSHIPS NOT AWARDED at DIVISION III: There is no uniform set of eligibility requirements for Division III schools. Eligibility for admission, financial aid, practice and competition is determined by the college or university.

NAIA ELIGIBILITY CENTER: Like the NCAA, the NAIA also requires all student-athletes to be certified through their Eligibility Center (www.PlayNAIA.org). Students will need to create a profile with their current contact information, high school information, as well as official ACT/SAT test results sent directly from the organizations and a copy of an official final transcript.

NAIA ACADEMIC STANDARDS:
If you will graduate from a U.S. high school this spring and enroll in college this coming fall, the requirements are simple. An entering freshman must:

#1- Be a graduate of an accredited high school or be accepted as a regular student in good standing as defined by the enrolling institution and

#2- Meet two of the three following requirements. If as an entering freshman you do not meet at least two of the three standards, you cannot participate in athletics for the first full year of attendance (2 semesters, 3 quarters, or equivalent).

NCAA RECRUIT TIPS: 7 STEPS TO A SCHOLARSHIP

MUST MEET TWO OF THE THREE
#1. TEST SCORE REQUIREMENT - Achieve a minimum of 18*** on the ACT or 860 [Critical Reading and Math] on the SAT (if taken before March 2016) or 940 SAT [Evidence-Based Reading and Writing + Math] if taken in March of 2016 or after)**.
#2. HIGH SCHOOL GPA REQUIREMENT - Achieve a minimum overall high school grade point average of 2.0 on a 4.0 scale.
#3. CLASS RANK REQUIREMENT- Graduate in the top half of your high school class.

** Students who scored between 860 and 930 on the March 2016 or later SAT test will be granted an automatic SAT test score minimum exception to compete during the 2016-17 academic year. The NAIA Eligibility Center will automatically apply this SAT test score minimum exception in the eligibility determination process. Learn more about this change.
*** Students who scored between 16 and 17 on the March 2016 or later ACT test will be granted an automatic ACT test score minimum exception to compete during the 2016-17 academic year. The NAIA Eligibility Center will automatically apply this ACT test score minimum exception in the eligibility determination process.

For home-schooled, GED graduates and International students, please visit www.playnaia.org for academic requirements!

NOTE: As an association, the NAIA does not have a letter of intent (LOI) program in which students sign a binding agreement to participate in athletics at a particular institution. Student-athletes may sign letters of intent with an individual NAIA school, however, they aren't obligated to attend that institution. That said, some NAIA conferences require their member schools to recognize letters of intent that are signed with other institutions within the conference. Please check with your prospective school to see if any conference programs apply. (From the NAIA).

STUDENTS WITH DOCUMENTED EDUCATION-IMPACTING DISABILITIES
From the NCAA... For academic eligibility purposes, the NCAA defines an education-impacting disability as a current impairment that has a substantial educational impact on a student's academic performance and requires accommodation.

Some of the most common EIDs:
- Learning disabilities or disorders.
- Attention deficit hyperactivity disorder.
- Mental health disorders. • Medical conditions.
- Deaf or hard of hearing.
- Autism spectrum disorder.

If you have a documented EID, you must meet the same initial-eligibility standards as other students but may be provided certain accommodations to help meet those standards. For instance, if you have a documented EID, you may be allowed to take classes designed for students with EIDs if the classes appear on the list of NCAA-approved courses at your school.

If you plan on attending a Division I school and your EID documentation is approved by the NCAA Eligibility Center, you may take up to three additional core courses after graduating from high school and before enrolling full time at a Division I school, as long as you graduate high school in eight consecutive semesters after starting ninth grade.

If you plan on attending a Division II school, you may take an unlimited number of core courses after starting ninth grade and before enrolling full time at a Division II school.

Submitting Your EID Documentation
If you are a student with a documented EID, you only need to alert the NCAA Eligibility Center to your EID if you are planning on enrolling full time at a Division I school and would like to take additional core courses after you graduate high school. Information about EIDs submitted to the NCAA is not released to colleges unless the student athlete makes a specific written request.

To document your EID with the NCAA Eligibility Center, you must submit the following materials:
1. A complete NCAA EID cover sheet.
2. Your NCAA identification number, high school graduation year, permanent address and phone number.
3. Current, signed documentation of your diagnosis (including test data) and/or recommendations from the treating professional (e.g., medical doctor, clinical psychologist or other qualified individual).
4. Current copy of your Individualized Education Program or Section 504 Plan. If your high school did not provide an IEP or 504 Plan, the high school must submit documentation describing the available accommodations or an explanation of why accommodations were not provided.
5. A signed Buckley statement form allowing certain individuals to review your EID information and speak on your behalf to the NCAA. A parent or guardian who would like to discuss your EID request with the NCAA must be listed on the Buckley statement.

The cover sheet and Buckley statement can be found at NCAA.org/playcollegesports.

Where To Send Your EID Documents
NCAA Eligibility Center
EID Services
P.O. Box 7110
Indianapolis, IN 46207-7110
Fax: 317-968-5100

NCAA RECRUIT TIPS: 7 STEPS TO A SCHOLARSHIP

Email: ec-processing@ncaa.org

If approved, you will be notified in writing and provided with additional information about available accommodations.

SAT/ACT Exam With Accommodations
If you have a documented EID, you may also request to take an SAT or ACT exam with accommodations to satisfy testscore requirements by:
- Registering for accommodations using the directions provided by the SAT or ACT.
- Follow procedures governed by SAT or ACT. The test may not be administered by a member of your high school athletics department or any NCAA school's athletics department.
- If you take an SAT or ACT exam with accommodations, you may take the test on a date other than a national testing date, but you still must achieve the required test score.
- Your high school counselor can help you register to take an SAT or ACT exam with accommodations.

Remember: You should complete your NCAA Eligibility Center registration before submitting your EID documentation.

DOCUMENTATION FOR HOME SCHOOL STUDENTS
From the NCAA... Learning at home is not necessarily the same as being home schooled. Because of recent growth in online and virtual education, a student may be able to learn at home through an online school with online teachers, which would not be considered a parent-directed home school.

Courses that will be evaluated as home school courses are those in which a parent or tutor:
- Plans and delivers actual instructional activities such as lectures, discussions, tutorials, feedback or assistance.
- Determines the student's comprehension of the material by grading and evaluating student performance and achievement on assignments and assessments and providing appropriate re-teaching and feedback.
- Determines the overall grade the student achieved in the course.
- Places the grade on a transcript or grade report or reports the grade to a transcription agency.

How to Register: If you are a home school student and want to play NCAA sports at a Division I or II school, you need to register with the NCAA Eligibility Center and meet the same standards as all other students.

Once you have completed your registration, you will want to go to NCAA.org/playcollegesports and visit the Home School Students section for a Tool Kit to provide you with necessary home school resources.

WHERE TO SEND YOUR HOME SCHOOL DOCUMENTS
All documents must be submitted to the following address:
NCAA Eligibility Center
(ATTN: Home School Evaluation)
1802 Alonzo Watford Sr. Drive
Indianapolis, IN 46202-6222

NCAA RECRUITING DEFINITIONS
Important Terms to Know From the NCAA Guide for the College-Bound Student Athlete...

Contact: A contact happens any time a college coach says more than hello during a face-to-face meeting with you or your parents off the college's campus.

Contact period: During a contact period, a college coach may have face-to-face contact with you or your parents, watch you compete or visit your high school and write or telephone you or your parents.

Dead period: A college coach may not have any face-to-face contact with you or your parents on or off the college campus at any time during a dead period. The coach may write and call you or your parents during this time.

Evaluation: An evaluation happens when a college coach observes you practicing or competing.

Evaluation period: During an evaluation period, a college coach may watch you compete, visit your high school and write or telephone you or your parents. However, a college coach may not have face-to-face contact with you or your parents off the college's campus during an evaluation period.

Financial aid: (scholarship) Any money you receive from a college or another source, such as outside loans or grants. Financial aid may be based on athletics ability, financial need or academic achievement.

Five-year clock: If you play at a Division I school, you have five-calendar years in which to play four seasons of competition. Your five-year clock starts when you enroll as a full-time student at any college. Thereafter, your clock continues, even if you spend an academic year in residence as a result of transferring, decide to redshirt, if you do not attend school or even if you go part time during your college career.

Official visit: During an official visit, the college can pay for transportation to and from the college for you, lodging and meals (Division I allows for up to three meals per day) for you and your parents or guardians, as well as reasonable entertainment expenses including three tickets to a Division I home sports event or five tickets to a Division II home sports event. Before a college may invite you on an official visit, you will have to provide the college with a copy of your high school transcript and ACT, SAT or PLAN score (test scores are required for Division I only) and register with the NCAA Eligibility Center.

Quiet period: During this time, a college coach may not have any in-person contact with you or your parents off the college's campus. The coach may not watch you play or visit your high school during this period. You and your parents may visit a college campus during this time. A coach may write or call you or your parents during this time.

Recruited: If a college coach calls you more than once, contacts you off campus, pays your expenses to visit the campus, or in Divisions I and II, issues you a National Letter of Intent or a written offer of financial aid, you are considered to be recruited.

Recruiting calendar: NCAA member schools limit recruiting to certain periods during the year. Recruiting calendars promote the well-being of college-bound student-athletes and ensure fairness among schools by defining certain periods during the year in which recruiting may or may not occur in a particular sport.

Season of competition: Generally, NCAA rules say that any competition in a season — regardless of the amount of time — counts as having played a season in that sport. If you play any time during a season, regardless of how long you played, it counts as having played for an entire season in that sport. Your season of competition starts when you spend one second in competition on the field, court, gym or track.

Ten-semester/15-quarter clock: If you play at a Division II or III school, you have the first 10 semesters or 15 quarters in which you are enrolled as a full-time student to complete your four seasons of participation. You use a semester or quarter any time you attend class as a full-time student or are enrolled part time and compete for the school. You do not use a term if you only attend part time with no competition or are not enrolled for a term.

Two-year college: An school where students can earn an Associate of Arts (AA) degree, an Associate of Science (AS) degree or an Associate of Applied Science degree within two years. Some people call these schools community colleges or junior colleges.

Unofficial visit: Any visit by you and your parents to a college campus paid for by you or your parents. The only expense you may receive from the college is three complimentary admissions to a Division I home athletics contest or five complimentary admissions to a Division II home athletics contest. You may make as many unofficial visits as you like and may take those visits at any time. The only time you cannot talk with a coach during an unofficial visit is during a dead period.

Verbal commitment: A verbal commitment happens when you verbally agree to play sports for a college before you sign or are eligible to sign a National Letter of Intent. The commitment is not binding on you or the school and can be made at any time.

Walk-on: Someone who is not typically recruited by a school to participate in sports and does not receive a scholarship from the school, but who becomes a member of one of the school's athletics teams.

ACTION STEPS: UNDERSTANDING MANDATORY REQUIREMENTS

- **UNDERSTANDING LEVELS OF OPPORTUNITIES: DIFFERENCE BETWEEN NCAA PROGRAMS (DI, DII, DIII), NAIA PROGRAMS & JUNIOR COLLEGE PROGRAMS:** YOUR TALENT AND THE COLLEGE COACHES WILL DETERMINE WHAT LEVEL YOU GET RECRUITED AT. IF YOU HAVEN'T RECEIVED ANY INTEREST YET, IT'S BEST TO KEEP AN OPEN MIND! YOU DON'T WANT TO TURN OPPORTUNITIES AWAY, ESPECIALLY EARLY IN THE PROCESS. THERE ARE HUNDREDS OF GREAT OPPORTUNITIES OUT THERE OUTSIDE OF JUST NCAA DIVISION I!

LEVEL OF COMPETITION: CIRCLE WHICH LEVELS HAVE SHOWN INTEREST:				
NCAA DI	NCAA DII	NCAA DIII	NAIA	JUCO

- **CORE COURSE GPA REQUIREMENTS:** ARE YOU FAMILIAR AND ON TRACK WITH THE CORE COURSES REQUIRED TO BE ADMITTED AND APPROVED THROUGH THE ELIGIBILITY CENTER? (CORE COURSE EXAMPLES: ENGLISH, MATH, NATURAL/PHYSICAL SCIENCE, SOCIAL SCIENCE, FOREIGN LANGUAGE, RELIGION, PHILOSOPHY.) – SEE PAGES 14-17 FOR REQUIREMENTS.

- **SLIDING SCALE REQUIREMENTS FOR SAT/ACT SCORES:** AS A JUNIOR, BEGIN TO TAKE THE ACT OR SAT TESTS TO GIVE YOURSELF TIME TO IMPROVE SCORES, IF NECESSARY, AS YOU GET CLOSER TO GRADUATION. ALWAYS BE AWARE OF THE COMBINATION OF MINIMUM SCORES NEEDED BETWEEN YOUR CORE COURSE GPA AND SAT/ACT TEST SCORES. SEE PAGE 14-17 FOR SCORE REQUIREMENTS.

- **REGISTERING WITH THE ELIGIBILITY CENTER:** AT THE END OF YOUR SOPHOMORE YEAR OR THE BEGINNING OF YOUR JUNIOR YEAR, REGISTER WITH THE NCAA AND/OR NAIA ELIGIBILITY CENTER. BEFORE YOU CAN ENROLL AT AN NCAA DI/DII OR NAIA INSTITUTION YOU MUST BE CLEARED THROUGH THEIR ELIGIBILITY CENTERS! BY REGISTERING EARLY, YOU CAN MAKE SURE THAT YOU ARE ON TRACK WITH ALL THE REQUIREMENTS AHEAD OF TIME AND BE AWARE OF ANY CHANGES THAT MAY GO INTO EFFECT.

SUBMIT TEST SCORES TO THE ELIGIBILITY CENTER: BE SURE TO REQUEST THAT YOUR ACT/SAT SCORES BE SENT DIRECTLY TO THE NCAA AND/OR NAIA ELIGIBILITY CENTER BEFORE YOU TAKE THE TEST BY USING THE CODE 9999 (NCAA) OR 9876 (NAIA)! THE ELIGIBILITY CENTER REQUIRES THAT SCORES BE SENT DIRECTLY, AND NOT TAKEN FROM TRANSCRIPTS. BY REQUESTING PRIOR TO TAKING THE EXAM, YOU WON'T HAVE TO PAY ADDITIONAL FEES TO HAVE THE SCORES SENT AFTER YOU TAKE THE TEST!

STEP #2
GETTING STARTED & GETTING NOTICED

"Never mistake activity for achievement."
– JOHN WOODEN

"No one said it would be easy, they just said it would be worth it."

"Impossible is not a fact. It is an opinion."
– MUHAMMAD ALI

"Don't wish it were easier, wish you were better."
– JIM ROHN

SCHOLARSHIP OFFERS: EARNED, NOT GIVEN

THE SCHOLARSHIP OFFER! What is the answer to the million dollar question—what can I do to put myself in the best position possible to get a collegiate athletic scholarship? Instead of starting this "how-to" at the very beginning with Step #1, I will start at the end, the moment that you are working so hard to get to! We're starting at the moment your phone rings, you answer it and the coach at your dream school says, "Hey, are you ready??? We'd love for you to be a part of our family! I was calling to offer you a scholarship... what do you say?"

First and foremost, scholarship offers are EARNED—they are not GIVEN. There is no promise or guarantee that a coach will offer you a scholarship, and it's definitely a process that will take you on an emotional roller coaster. You'll laugh, you'll cry... heck, you may even pee your pants as one recruit did during my time helping coordinate official visits! Before you get too deep in the process I just want you to respect the fact that scholarship offers are EARNED and that you are going to have to prepare yourself to go out there and be in the best position to "earn it!" So here we go...

COACHES ARE LOOKING FOR SKILL, SIZE, SPEED, TOUGHNESS, LEADERSHIP, A RELENTLESS ATTITUDE AND GREAT GRADES.

Nothing is remotely official until a school gives you a written or verbal scholarship offer, preferably a written one! You may be getting a ton of cards, emails and Twitter DMs but a coach must give you an OFFER for you to know that they are 100% interested in you. If they haven't offered you a scholarship or tried to get you to campus for a visit (Unofficial or Official), they're not completely sold on you yet. They may be calling you or sending you mail but they're still just keeping an eye on you... they've heard about you somehow and are starting their research on you!

To many high school players, it seems as if teammates and other players in the area are getting new offers every day, that they just fall from the sky for everyone else. Understand that coaches put a LOT of time and research into making the decision to pull the trigger and offer a player a scholarship. In most cases, they've scouted your video, watched you in person at multiple games, discussed it as a staff in depth and have been making calls to their sources in your area to find out more about you as a player and student and more importantly, as a person. They have evaluated your strengths, weaknesses, attitude, coachability, where you fit into their style of play and if you can get into school academically.

They ask themselves, "Do we have a shot with any other players who are more talented?" (Hey, you wanted me to be honest, right? That's what they're thinking.)

NCAA RECRUIT TIPS: 7 STEPS TO A SCHOLARSHIP

The highest compliment a school can give you is to offer you a scholarship, so be very appreciative of the achievement. This means that they see something in you that they believe in- believe me, they've done their homework! By the end of the process, you just need ONE coaching staff to believe in you, not 50! So when that moment happens, appreciate it!

It's also important to understand that even if you've made a national or statewide Top 100 recruiting list, that doesn't mean that every college and university will automatically offer you a scholarship. Coaches will be extra diligent in their research, no matter how many ranking lists you are on. The only ranking that they care about is their OWN evaluation of your play, not what every internet blogger thinks!

Most head coaches want someone on their staff to see you play in person before extending the scholarship offer, and they usually prefer to see you play in person for themselves as well. If the head coach isn't able to get there to see you play, they often send a second assistant coach out to cross-check the first coaches' evaluations and what your highlights and game film showed. The coaching staff will discuss your abilities and attitude with your prep coaches, coaches who you regularly play against, family and their trusted sources in your area to determine if you are truly the real deal before they extend the offer!

FEARS DISAPPEAR WHEN YOU PREPARE. IT'S FUNNY HOW IT WORKS: WHEN YOU PREPARE AND CHALLENGE YOURSELF ON THE HIGHEST LEVEL YOUR FEARS WILL DISAPPEAR.

It's important that you never put an expiration date on your dream of getting a scholarship or the chance to play college sports. Too often, players get frustrated early in the process and don't go FIND their opportunities. Life happens for those people who go out and MAKE it happen!

Always have faith in yourself, work hard every single day and stay positive while working towards that big chance! I've worked with several coaches who offered players a scholarship just days or hours before Signing Day. Rosters and commitments from other players are fluid – understand it's an unpredictable process, that nothing is final and to be patient! There are plenty of Plan B's, Plan C's and Plan D's that can keep your dream of playing college sports alive!

The recruiting process has the power to turn some players into monsters, and others into an insecure, miserable mess. I'm here to tell you to RELAX... STAY POSITIVE... and HAVE FUN!

If you aren't an internet sensation with 50 offers to pick from, understand that you just need ONE! You just have to find that ONE coach who will believe in you and give you a chance!

ODDS OF PLAYING NCAA AFTER HIGH SCHOOL
Having the opportunity to become an NCAA athlete, scholarship or walk-on player, is an honor. Only a small percentage of high school players actually move on to compete at the NCAA level, by sport:

- Football: 6.5%
- Men's Basketball: 3.4%
- Women's Basketball: 3.8%
- Baseball: 6.9%
- Men's Soccer: 5.7%
- Men's Ice Hockey: 11.2%

#1 RULE TO GET NOTICED
The #1 rule to memorize heading into this process is that in order for a coach to be interested in recruiting you, they MUST see you play—either in person or on video.

Remind yourself of this over and over every time you find yourself frustrated with the process. We will be going over this in depth shortly and you will be learning multiple ways to make this happen but it is the principle I want you to keep coming back to—COACHES MUST SEE YOU PLAY IN ORDER TO BE 100% INTERESTED!

THE FIRST QUESTION COACHES WILL ASK YOU
You finally get a college coach on the phone or in front of you! You are halfway there! After the introductions and small talk, one of the first questions that they will ask you is, "What other schools have offered you?" PAUSE. Don't worry, there are no wrong answers to this. Some of you may say, "Texas, North Carolina, Virginia Tech, Syracuse, Florida State and a few others I can't remember." Others may say "Elon and James Madison," "Temple, Rice, Sacramento State," or "Western Carolina, North Carolina A&T, Florida Atlantic." And even more recruits may say, "Nobody yet."

Remember—there is no wrong answer to this question. It's like the chicken or the egg debate, SOMEONE has to be the first to offer you! Hey, maybe one day it will be this coach you are talking to!

This quickly gives coaches a good idea of your ability, it's a reference point for them. If other schools have already done their research on you and found SOMETHING in you, your 'dream' school may be more willing to take a look too. But, even if you have no offers—that doesn't mean they'll immediately reject you—they will probably just ask you to submit a highlight video or invite you to camp.

Never lie about what scholarship offers you have because coaches can find out within minutes, and it will only eliminate you from their list if they catch you in a lie. Coaches DO double-check your offers, usually the minute they hang up the phone!

The next thing college coaches will want to know (especially if you have no offers) is which schools have tried to get you to campus for an unofficial visit or camp, or which programs have come to see you (not one of your teammates) play or practice. Remember—just because you haven't been OFFERED, that doesn't mean other schools may not be INTERESTED. Coaches may still be doing their research on you, so other coaches who you are reaching out to may ask you which schools are scouting you, inviting you to unofficial visits, Junior Days or camps.

Be up front but never make excuses! The worst thing you can do at this point is lie or give coaches a long list of why-nots... "the coach hates me," "my mom hates me," "my team sucks." Even if your coach hates you, your mom is trying to interfere with the process and your team didn't win a game last year—never start making excuses! Ever!

If you haven't had much contact or feedback from college coaches, get some exposure at regional or national combines or tournaments. Give coaches a list of past and future events that you have or will attend, and they will be able to get an idea of your talent level from those invites as well.

FRUSTRATION IS NATURAL. THE QUESTION IS: HOW LONG WILL YOU LET THAT BITTERNESS EAT YOU UP? USE ITS POWER TO MOTIVATE!

Don't bother with the, "see what happened was..." and just tell the coaches the truth—"I'm just now starting to reach out to schools, here is my highlight video, stats and contact info, can you take a look and let me know what you think?" Period, skip the rest!

STUDENT-ATHLETE RESUME
Along with being seen, you will need to put together a Student-Athlete Resume, your profile that will give coaches a quick look at your accomplishments, measurements and contact information. Putting together this profile will be one of your first priorities, a task that you will need to do BEFORE you begin to reach out to coaches.

There are two examples on the next page to use as you format your information. When including accomplishments or stats, be sure to put the most impressive notes on top. Coaches and staff can get hundreds of these each week, they may be scanning piles of these, and if your highlights aren't jumping off the page in 20 seconds, they'll likely move on to the next player.

@1001RecruitTips

SAMPLE #1: STUDENT-ATHLETE RESUME

NAME

#Jersey Number - (YEAR) - Position Height / Weight / Speed
High School (City, ST) Phone # / Email Address
HOME ADDRESS: Home Mailing Address, City, St, Zip

ATHLETIC ACCOMPLISHMENTS: (All-State, All-Conference, Team MVP, School Record, Stat Leader)
ATHLETIC STATS: (Top 4-5 Sport-Specific Stats) ACADEMIC INFO: GPA / ACT Test Score / SAT Test Score / PSAT Test Score

HS Coach Name (HS Coach Cell #/HS Coach Email) High School Name – High School Address, St, Zip
AAU Team Name
AAU Coach Name (AAU Coach Cell #/AAU Coach Email)

ACADEMIC INFO: GPA / ACT Score / SAT Score

SAMPLE #2: STUDENT-ATHLETE RESUME

MICHAEL SMITH

#98- (2019) – Defensive End
6'4 / 240 / 4.85
Thomas Jefferson HS (Honolulu, HI)
222-555-5555 / MichaelSmith98@gmail.com
Twitter and Instagram: @MikeSmith98
HOME ADDRESS: 105 Main Street, Honolulu, HI 55225

ATHLETIC ACCOMPLISHMENTS:
Named 1st Team All-County by Hawaii Times
Team Defensive MVP
Lead the conference in sacks (15) and PBU (9)
ATHLETIC STATS:
Junior Season: 15 sacks, 9 PBU, 4 TFL, 2 INT
Sophomore Season: 9 sacks, 2 PBU, 7 TFL, 1 INT

ACADEMIC INFO: 3.5 GPA / 81 ACT score / 1020 SAT Score

HS Coach: Coach Kevin Johnson - 222-555-7777 / CoachKJohnson@yahoo.com
Thomas Jefferson HS – 1500 South Street, Honolulu, HI 55225

NCAA RECRUIT TIPS: 7 STEPS TO A SCHOLARSHIP

DON'T PAY SERVICES TO GET YOUR NAME OUT TO RECRUITERS

Here is a tip to save you a few bucks—Never pay a recruiting service to send your information to universities, especially larger Division I schools.
First off, this book will teach you to find the contact information that you need and to put together your own Student-Athlete Resume and highlight video.

Secondly, particularly at competitive Division I programs, stacks of athlete resumes aren't taken serious or even looked at in most cases. If you have to pay someone to send out your profile, you must not be that talented. True or not, that is the impression it gives off.

Put together your Student-Athlete Resume, your highlight video and mail and email them off to the schools that interest you. You can find all the contact information that you need within a few clicks online. And, coaches like players who can show SOME initiative and do some of this work on their own.

DIVISION I, II, III, JUCO, NAIA... YOU CAN FIND GREAT COACHES, TEAMMATES AND EXPERIENCES ON EVERY LEVEL! GO WHERE YOU ARE WANTED, HAPPY AND HAVE OPPORTUNITIES!

Personally, I would discredit these resumes that were paid for and sent in bulk, and very few coaches actually looked at them or added their information to their watch list or to the database. From my experience at FBS Division I schools, I don't remember a coach handing me one to add that prospects' info to the database, ever! But they often handed me ones that players, parents or prep coaches had put together themselves to add to their own watch list.

Sure, they were used more at some of the small programs that I worked with but players would have gotten the same responses if they would have mailed in their own letter and resume. Send it on your own and they will be more likely to read it! Those companies have no extra leverage that you don't have yourself!

START LOCAL

Since one of the first questions a coach will ask you is "Who have you been offered by?" you'll be taken much more seriously if you can give them some names! If coaches know that you already have offers, it tells them that you have some level of talent and other coaches have already done some research on you.

It's much more efficient to start with smaller programs and potentially work your way up to more competitive programs than by starting the process trying to chase around the defending national champions for an offer. Start small first, then if you are getting positive feedback—go bigger (if that's your dream).

All coaches keep an eye on good local and state players—so if a certain recruit is getting a lot of mid-major attention, there's a good chance that some of the bigger schools may come do their research too.

Too often, I would get calls about players who had no offers at all— that's just a waste of everyone's time. It will be much easier for you to get your foot in the door with UNC, NC State, Wake Forest and Duke if you are a prep player from North Carolina and getting offers from UNC-Wilmington, Western Carolina, Catawba and North Carolina A&T.

Coaches want to recruit the best talent they can find—players that other schools usually have interest in too.

Once you begin to get feedback from coaches about what level you can compete at, check out multiple schools at that level. Build momentum, continue to play hard and potentially work your way to other, more competitive schools that interest you if you dream of playing major college sports.

Personally, I attended a small school that was Division II (I-AA football at the time) when I enrolled, and I had the best four years of my life there. Don't eliminate smaller schools who are interested in you, you may be missing out on a once-in-a-lifetime experience!

SACRIFICES ARE NOT PUNISHMENTS, THEY ARE INVESTMENTS! INVEST BIG TO WIN BIG, YOU HAVE TO SACRIFICE CONSISTENTLY!

TOP 100 LISTS:
IF YOU ARE NOT RANKED, IT ISN'T THE END OF THE WORLD OR EVEN A SETBACK THAT WILL PREVENT YOU FROM EARNING SEVERAL SCHOLARSHIP OFFERS

NCAA RECRUIT TIPS: 7 STEPS TO A SCHOLARSHIP

UNDERSTAND THIS:

A COLLEGE COACH WILL RARELY JUST SHOW UP AT YOUR SCHOOL AND 'DISCOVER' YOU....

THERE IS A METHOD TO THE MADNESS:

Coaches and programs build their specific 'watch lists' of recruitable junior and senior high school players, and these lists will start to be compiled as early as your freshman year in high school, years before coaches are able to contact or recruit you.

This 'watch list' is their base list, an incomplete list. Circumstances will change from the time coaches may add you to their watch list to when they may begin reaching out to you until you sign that NLI in front of all of your family and friends. These watch lists are fluid and can change daily!
This chapter is devoted to all players—from national Top 100 players to hopeful athletes who may not be getting a lot of attention from coaches by their junior or senior year.

It will never be easy and in most cases, you will have several doors slammed in your face. You WILL have plenty of unanswered phone calls and emails, but I promise these temporary setbacks and hurdles will lead you to the team you are meant to play for. You want to find a team that needs and wants a player just like you! Let's go!

THE OBSTACLES THAT YOU FACE ARE STOPPING MOST OTHER PLAYERS TOO. WHEN YOU OVERCOME THEM, YOU TAKE A STEP AHEAD OF THE PACK TO SEPERATE YOURSELF!

8 REASONS WHY PLAYERS MAY BEGIN TO BE RECRUITED

Players may begin to be recruited by college coaches if they...

#1: Were named as a great player by a reputable scouting service on a national or regional report that the coaches subscribe to

#2: Had impressive regional or national combine results (height, weight, speed, vertical, stats, notes) that were sent to the coaches

#3: Were an impressive player at a tournament or game where college coaches were scouting

#4: Were recommended by your high school or AAU coach, especially if your coach has had success throughout their career or has an established relationship with particular college coaches

#5: Stood out as a great player at a college or university camp

#6: Sent a highlight or game video to the coaches and they were impressed

#7: Were offered by a rival or comparable school within the conference or region

#8: Political ties (a best friend of a top recruit or family member of an influential person within the University or Athletic Department)

CHAMPIONS DON'T USUALLY WIN ON THE 1ST EFFORT— IT'S ABOUT FIGHTING THROUGH TO YOUR 2ND, 3RD, 4TH, 5TH, 6TH TRY. KEEP TRYING, KEEP FIGHTING FOR WHAT YOU WANT IN LIFE!

8 REASONS WHY PLAYERS MAY BEGIN TO BE RECRUITED

#1: Were named as a great player by a reputable scouting service on a national or regional report that the coaches subscribe to

As we will discuss in detail in the next few pages, coaches can find out about you in several different ways. One of the easiest ways that they may get your name and contact information is through national or regional scouting services. These services generate reports from particular regions, events or the ever-popular Top 100 internet rankings.

Being rated in the national or state Top 100 by a fan media site can be a gift and a curse for many athletes. Such rankings may help get your name out there to more coaches but it may also provide you with a false sense of security.

If you happen to be named to such ranks, understand that these lists are only a starting point for most coaches. It may put you on their radar or 'watch list' but it doesn't guarantee scholarship offers or starting jobs. Understand that these Top 100 lists change often and understand that your ranking will definitely rise or fall during this process!

On a yearly basis, I've sat in recruiting meetings as our staff would go through Top 100 lists from popular internet sites and disagree with their rankings on many players. Oftentimes, one assistant coach reads off the names and the other assistant coaches respond with "overrated," "ehhhh," "a beast," "overrated," "slow," "good but not tough." You may be impressing fans who waste their days on the blogs but not necessarily impressing the coaches who are extending the scholarship offers. Coaches do their own complete evaluations and your internet ranking plays zero influence on their thoughts of you as a prospective student-athlete!

THERE ARE THOUSANDS OF PLAYERS OUT THERE TRYING TO TAKE THE SAME SCHOLARSHIP THAT YOU ARE DREAMING OF. YOU MUST OUTWORK THOSE PLAYERS EVERY DAY.

Coaches use these lists as a starting point. They often drop a few of these 'Top 100' prospects off their watch list after seeing them play in person, or they may prefer one of their teammates or unknown players that they are competing against instead and add them. They may go out and see a highly-recruited internet player and find them too small, slow, out-of-condition, soft or uncoachable and cut them from their list.

Of course, the top three or four players nationally DO usually make an impact earlier in their career but not necessarily everyone else... coaches don't care if you are #26 or #98... or even unranked. They really could care less about your internet ranking!

Other, less public, recruiting services send scouting reports in nearly every sport and geographic region. Most major programs may subscribe to 10 or more of these types of services. Just because a coach with a school-logoed polo isn't sitting in the stands, that doesn't mean that there isn't anyone there watching and taking notes. Coaches get tips about players everywhere, it just depends on if it's a source that particular coach knows or trusts. Coaches depend on these services to help start their research, especially for the key contact information and evaluations they may provide on freshman and sophomore players!

There are likely independent scouts in your region that put together ranking lists for each grade in the area, and sell these lists to several universities. Most scouts include notes (10 words to a paragraph) about your strengths and weaknesses, along with your height, weight, school and contact info. More importantly, they list each player with a recommendation or ranking— DI, DII, DIII, NAIA. Schools use the rankings to separate elite players from good ones, and the good players from the average ones.

At every school and in nearly every sport I've worked in, schools use these reports to find prospects for their level of completion. Reports are generated from everywhere—Mississippi, Kansas, Georgia, Florida, New England, Texas, Illinois, Southern California, Northern California, Junior Colleges and on International players.

For example, basketball scouting reports will list players as High Major+, High Major, High Major-, Mid-Major+, Mid-Major, Mid-Major-, Low-Major+, Low Major, Low Major-, Division II, Division III or NAIA. Coaches determine what level their school fits on and will look into prospects that fall into their range. They'll add those names to their prospect database, send out a questionnaire, keep an eye out while on the road, maybe request their highlight video. They may call your coach for

HOW HARD YOU WORK WHEN NOBODY IS WATCHING OR KEEPING SCORE WILL DETERMINE HOW SUCCESSFUL YOU BECOME!

more information and to find out their thoughts. Remember, these lists are just recommendations and really just a starting point for coaches until they can get out to see you play in person for themselves.

Staffs also cross-reference juniors and seniors on these regional reports to make sure that they haven't missed any late-bloomers or transplanted upperclassmen who have recently moved into the region. Again, the real value in these reports is often in finding the talented freshman and sophomores early or in building a complete list of potential players in the state. Coaches work a year or two ahead in the process and keep an early eye on these top prospects. The earlier they can evaluate these younger players and build relationships with their team and coaches, the better.

NCAA RECRUIT TIPS: 7 STEPS TO A SCHOLARSHIP

If you aren't ranked nationally, it isn't the end of the world or even a setback that will prevent you from earning numerous scholarship offers. If you are a junior and aren't earning offers, it's not the end of the world either—it just means you will have to put in footwork over the summer to get your name out there.

Having been within earshot of daily non-stop recruiting calls, I would hear college coaches ask prep coaches often, "Hey, so tell me who's a great player in your area that nobody's talking about." Coaches don't care about the shine, they care about the talent, passion, size and speed... and they want to be the first to discover that hidden gem and they're asking everyone! They leave no stone unturned.

PLAYERS THAT MAKE CONSISTENT PLAYS THROUGHOUT GAMES ARE THE REAL GAME-CHANGERS, NOT JUST THE ONES WHO FOCUS ON MAKING THAT ONE ESPN-TYPE PLAY.

If you are rated #1 in the country or #10 in your school, keep playing hard, training hard and focusing on developing your leadership skills! Ignore your ranking because they play NO influence on whether a school will offer you a scholarship or not! Truly.

College coaches are always looking for great players, but even more desirable is finding great players who are leaders on winning teams. They want players who have a taste of winning and know what it feels like to be successful. It is something repeated over and over during evaluations, "We want great players who are winners." I've heard that from coaches at nearly every school, in every sport. If you focus more time on your fundamentals and improving your team than your internet ranking—success will come. If you are a top team in the state, scouts will come. If you can lead your team to several wins or a state or conference title, it only adds to your chances of being noticed or offered a scholarship.

8 REASONS WHY PLAYERS MAY BEGIN TO BE RECRUITED
#2: Had impressive regional or national combine results (height, weight, speed, vertical, stats, notes) that were sent to the coaches

How do you stack up versus other players in your county, conference and state? Think a smaller version of the NFL combine, if all players were put in a room, separated by position, measured up and put through the same drills, players will begin separating themselves from top to bottom. Attending regional combines will help you get more exposure versus quality players in your area and will especially give you the chance to see how you stack up with measureables. In many sports, size and speed will help get you added to coaches' watch lists without them even knowing about your skill level.

Third-party organizations coordinate combines, showcases and tournaments across the country. From each site, players' heights, weights, speed, vertical jumps, contact info and other measureables are collected. A detailed report from each location (Orlando, Atlanta, Houston, Los Angeles, etc) is sent through a scouting service to coaches at programs across the country, including phone numbers, emails and mailing addresses for each combine participant. Each staff takes the data from each location and will add players to their watch lists accordingly based on their needs. Top measureables (height, weight, speed) are keys to being added to FBS/FCS schools, quality regional players are also taken into consideration from each area.

The key benefit about events like the Nike and Under Armour football combines are that they put your name and contact info out there to a variety of coaches. This is EXACTLY what you need if you think you have the skills and want to get noticed. It puts your verified, black and white measureables on a spreadsheet for coaches, along with your direct contact info! That's about as good as it gets, especially if coaches haven't been able to see you yet.

If you truly want to be successful, use these combines or exposure events as a measuring stick during your freshman or sophomore years. This should motivate you to begin to do the extra work that is necessary to be a great college player down the road. These events will be a wake-up call to you that either you need to work harder or they may be a confidence boost that should encourage you to strive for even more, to continue to separate yourself as one of the best. These events will help you get a better idea of where you fit in. Participating in these events at an early age will help you prepare for the common drills that you will be put through during your collegiate career and will help you get over first-time jitters so that when you come back as a junior or senior you know exactly what is expected! You will know exactly what will be asked of you. Don't put too much pressure on yourself at these events but understand there is value in working extremely hard and preparing for these physical tests.

Coaches are always looking for players with the best position- specific skills, but size and speed are base traits that can also help you get on the map. Combines are just one way to get you on the map, but a quick way if you have the right measureables.

NAIA SHOWCASES: Many third-party organizations offer showcase opportunities for a variety of sports. The NAIA offers their own showcases around the country for a variety of sports including football, women's soccer, men's soccer, men's basketball, women's basketball, baseball and softball. For more information, visit www.naiashowcase.com.

NCAA RECRUIT TIPS: 7 STEPS TO A SCHOLARSHIP

8 REASONS WHY PLAYERS MAY BEGIN TO BE RECRUITED
#3: Were an impressive player at a tournament or game where college coaches were scouting

What separates good prep players from great ones is how they perform versus other players in head-to-head competitions. Sounds like common sense—know that you may be the superstar on varsity as a freshman at your school but unchallenged playing with and against weaker competition. How will you compete versus talented players in your area, how will you compete versus older and more physically developed players? Will you outperform them or will you be dominated? Put all of the players from your state in the ring, players will quickly begin separating themselves. Put those top players from each state in competition versus the best players from the 6-10 states within your region, a handful of players will really separate themselves, and that's the group that elite FBS schools will begin to go after.

While many prospects feel their only shot at getting discovered or recruited is if a college coach shows up at their school to watch a game, it's really not that common. First, coaches need a REASON to come to your school to scout you.

Combines will help you get on the map if you have good speed or size; competitions, events and tournaments will help you get noticed for your skill and technique as well.

In many sports, it is very helpful to play in AAU and compete in regional and national tournaments. These are the events that college coaches put priority on to scout. They bring several players in one location, giving coaches a few days to see a ton of prospects. If possible, try to get on a team and get out there to be seen at these events! That will only improve your chances to get them to come out to your school or to begin to recruit you. Remember, they need a REASON to come see you.

NCAA rules change every year, usually with the intent to limit college coaches to very select evaluation periods. A common complaint coaches have is that these strict rules make it difficult for coaches to get enough good looks at a prospect in action, in person. They may feel that it's not enough time to gather complete information about several players that they are recruiting. Therefore, the system has evolved into third-party events including AAU tournaments and 7-on-7 football tournaments, events that coaches can attend in-person or receive reports or results on.

Coaches know that you may have one or two bad games or practices when they are in attendance. They may hesitate to cut you from their watch list, or they may want to make sure that those one or two beastmode games that you had when they were in attendance weren't a fluke either. So the more they can see (or hear about) you competing with other great players, or the more concrete research that they can get on you from trusted events, the better.

In many sports, combines and tournaments can attract a range of talent and can create these head-to-head competitions that help coaches in the evaluation process. These events are organized to provide opportunities for coaches to sit back, watch and evaluate several players within a weekend.

Others events are organized to provide concrete measurements, scouting reports, results and contact information on several prospects to universities across the country, even if coaches are unable to be in attendance to due to NCAA rules. In any way possible, these events provide "exposure" to many prospects and help them get their name out.

> **IT'S NOT ABOUT YOUR POTENTIAL, IT'S ABOUT YOUR PRODUCTION. HOW DO YOU HELP YOUR TEAM? WHAT DO YOU BRING BESIDES YOUR STATS?**

It's important to compare yourself to other athletes your age and outwork those players. THIS is your competition. These are the players who want the same scholarships that you want. These are the hundreds of players calling, emailing and showing up on campus with the same dreams that you have. You have to find a way to separate yourself!

Be prepared to compete versus better talent and look for the best competition that you can find! Even if you don't match-up, it should motivate you to work harder and understand where you rank. It will pump those competitive juices and eventually you may become just as great as those players who are used to edging you talent-wise.

The drawback during some of these evaluations periods is that coaches have a very limited window of days they can scout these events across the country—too many games in too many locations in a very short period of time. They may already have their list of players that need to be scouted that they are making it a priority to see.

Also, once coaches have evaluated their top prospects, they often follow these prospects and show up at as many of their games as possible, even if their evaluations are done. So as an unknown player, your window is smaller than you think. Time is already devoted to just showing up to games of players that have already commited, or who are a priority to the head coach.

Each sport limits the number of contacts and evaluations coaches may make per prospect throughout the academic year. Each sport has further regulations about when, where and how often coaches may come evaluate you or meet with you, ask your coach or check with the NCAA. Understand that they are limited in the amount of times they may come watch you!

NCAA RECRUIT TIPS: 7 STEPS TO A SCHOLARSHIP

Coaches from every single university are traveling from Atlanta to Kentucky to Las Vegas to Los Angeles to Orlando to Philadelphia to evaluate players during evaluation periods. Coaches from the defending national champions will be at these tournaments... along with staffs from Top 25 schools, from mid-level programs and from teams that may have only won a couple games last year. Every coach is looking for talent, and looking for players that are passionate about playing.

These types of tournaments and evaluation periods are common for all college coaches—all sports. Coaches at the schools that you are interested in may not have the time or flexibility to get to your game if you aren't on their radar already. That's why it's important to try to get on their radar early, to give you more opportunities to be scouted.

> **HAVING DOUBT IS NATURAL, WHAT MAKES US HUMAN IS THE ABILITY TO OVERCOME OUR FEARS THROUGH HARD WORK AND HAVING A PLAN.**

For example, during a men's basketball evaluation period, I know of a coaching staff who went to one city for two tournaments that had 996 combined games scheduled over a three-day period on 47 different courts across town. The first game started at 8am and the last game started at 9:45pm. Almost 1,000 games in three days on 47 courts, you can't imagine the planning and coordination that goes into outlining the most important games to get to and putting together a schedule to make sure that they were getting to see the maximum amount of prospects! Coaches aren't just going to wander aimlessly at these events, they have a specific list of players to scout and a schedule to stick to. They may notice other players while scouting specific recruits but they may not have the time to just wander aimlessly to find players. They have to have a plan!

Each AAU tournament sells coaches a packet of information with participating player's names and contact info, as well as all the contact info for their AAU coaches. It works simply: when coaches see your talent and are interested, they add you to their list and get in contact with you or your coach. Watch lists undergo a major overhaul during these evaluation periods—cutting several players based on mediocre play, bad attitudes and size issues and adding even more players based on their talent, size, relentlessness and ability to make plays. They aren't just adding scorers, they're looking for defenders, rebounders, ball handlers and players who have a knack for making things happen. They'll come back from these events with thick books of rosters—hopefully with several names circled to add to the database.

Don't focus on your stat line at these events, focus on playing fundamentally solid and hustling on every play. For example, in basketball it's not as much about scoring 40 points in every game as it is about playing fundamentally sound. Don't put too much pressure on yourself to finish with a triple-double, instead you should focus on playing defense, getting rebounds, minimizing turnovers, hustling for loose balls and being a leader. For coaches, it's about finding the most consistent, toughest and fundamentally sound players who play hard and make a difference for their team, especially playing against the greatest competition. They aren't looking for ball hogs. You want to stand out as a difference-maker, what skill can you become a specialist at that will bring value to your team, to a potential college team, that can help you stand out?

When you are the hardest worker, a competitor and a leader at these events... coaches will notice.

8 REASONS WHY PLAYERS MAY BEGIN TO BE RECRUITED
#4: *Were recommended by your high school or AAU coach, especially if your coach has had success throughout their career or has an established relationship with particular college coaches*

A good place to start during your junior or senior year is with your high school and AAU coaches, they could be a valuable resource to you.

Get their opinion on what level you are most likely going to get looks from—in football are you an elite FBS player, Top 25, FBS- conference caliber, FCS, Division II, Division III or NAIA. In basketball, are you a high-major player, mid-major, low-major, Division II, Division III or NAIA material? In ANY sport, ask your coaches where they see you playing at the collegiate level.

If you are a senior, a player who had a serious injury or if you aren't able to qualify academically, are you a player who might do better going to a Junior College first for a year or two?

If your coaches have the same vision that you do and are willing to help, put together a list of the schools that you are interested in and ask them to send your highlight video and to call the recruiting coaches from those schools to get a read on their interest. Again, get the recruiting coaches name, direct phone number and email address—do the research for your coaches if they are willing to call for you.

Established prep coaches usually have connections with college coaches in the area. If your coach has been at the school for a few years, they've probably built up relationships with college coaches that have recruited that school in the past. If they've been coaching for awhile, they've got connections.

Most college coaches are receptive when high school coaches call about a specific player; especially if you play in a program that has had success or if

NCAA RECRUIT TIPS: 7 STEPS TO A SCHOLARSHIP

you are a player from the state. It's good business for college coaches to accept and return phone calls from any and every prep coach and most will if they have the time. Use this gesture of goodwill to your advantage and see if your coach can help you get your foot in the door. There is a decent chance that they can get through to the college coaches and get an honest evaluation on your chances of playing for that school, maybe quicker than if you call yourself. Remember, you need to be realistic and take the recommendation that your coaches give you about the conferences you might fit into.

Remember, this is all just a starting point. Too many players (and their families) get too offended during the process way too early— nothing is ever a final rejection! Thousands of players are underestimated every year and told they belong in less competitive programs than they may actually end up in. You can still keep your dreams alive for playing for Duke Basketball or Alabama Football but you're making a career-threatening decision if you don't at least follow the leads that you may have in the early stages through your high school or AAU coaches.

A prep coach shouldn't make a call to a school that is out-of-reach for you. Prep coaches want college coaches to respect their opinion and won't stick their neck out for you if you really don't have a shot to play for that program. You and your coach want to be taken serious.

From my experiences in major FBS programs, players have come into my office who wouldn't likely get offers from the local YMCA 30- year-old-and-up league. I would smile, nod my head and send them out the door with my business card. It's important to have dreams but it's also just as important to have a realistic back-up plan. It never hurts to start by checking out every school in a 300-mile radius.

One of the most critical things to remember is this—don't give control of your recruitment to anyone. Don't get in a situation where you must rely on your current coach for all of your communication and information from college coaches, especially if you are getting interest from several schools. It's nice of your prep coaches to offer to help you but don't let them become your decision-maker, wheeler- and-dealer or personal agent. When you give someone else the control, you open the door to NCAA violations. You will never hear the full story about which schools are interested in you and how strongly these schools are considering you because your 'mentor' may be getting a benefit or reward by steering you to a particular school.

Most prep coaches simply want to help you with the process, while others want to steer you to a particular school for favors or for their personal gain. They don't always have your best interest in mind. If your coaches are trying to put up a wall of communication between you and NCAA coaches and

insist that everyone goes through them, unfortunately they don't have your best interest in mind. That's your first red flag! A giant red flag!
Prep coaches are a great contact for college coaches but they aren't always helpful to all programs and opportunities that may be available to you.

Recruiting has always been political, and especially in today's climate of bazillion-dollar contracts and marketing deals, some prep coaches want to maximize their power—even if it's not beneficial to you. A small number of coaches are just looking out for themselves, which is exactly why I've written this book TO YOU as a prep player. I want YOU to be able to understand the system to eliminate your dependence on a coach serving as a middle-man (or woman!) for you.

JUST BECAUSE A COACH ISN'T AT YOUR GAME THAT DOESN'T MEAN SOMEONE ISN'T WATCHING! ESPECIALLY UNDERCLASSMAN, PEOPLE ARE WATCHING! LOTS OF OPPORTUNITIES!

Over the years I've heard several prep coaches talk about "owing a coach a player" or that they "only deal with a few coaches," as if they are making the complete decision for their player. This happens often, and is THE problem.

Being in the circle of an elite athlete puts many people in power positions for the first time in their lives. Some try to act like they are more powerful in the decision than the actual player—RED FLAG!

Every year I would run into numerous players who didn't know our school was interested in them until later in the process because their high school or AAU coaches were unwilling to help provide us with their direct contact info. There are several high school coaches who hide mail from select colleges because they have relationships with coaches at rival universities. It happens all the time and it's not fair to you! It is your right to be aware of EVERY opportunity available to you.

You must ALWAYS stay in control! Each extra layer of "people" coaches must get through is just another opportunity for you to be taken advantage of. YOU will face the suspensions and penalties, not your "people." And most of these characters who claim to be your "people" aren't near as powerful as you think, they may just gain power since coaches know they must go through them to get to you. YOU are the one with the power, no one else.

Lean on your coaches early in the process to help navigate the system. Ask for their advice. But under no circumstance should you ever put them in control of your decision or allow them to be the only point person for you.

You could end up in bad situations or be suspended by the NCAA when you aren't responsible for the process yourself. Even if you are shy or scared or have no other family members, never give control of the situation to anyone!

NCAA RECRUIT TIPS: 7 STEPS TO A SCHOLARSHIP

For as many great coaches that I know and have worked with, I would never tell ANYONE where they should go to school and who they should play for. Nobody but YOU should be making that decision based on where you are comfortable.

Keep it simple. The media and marketing companies have made the process a much more pressure-filled situation than it actually needs to be. If you have talent, you can get recruited by your play, not by someone being your agent. You don't need anyone to "sell" you to a university, to "pitch" you to coaches. The only thing college coaches can judge you on is seeing you play in person or on video. No high school coach or mentor can get a better chance for you in the recruiting process just by their endorsement—but they CAN help get your foot in the door by making a call and sending your highlight video.

The key to this process is simply a matter of getting an EVALUATION OF YOUR PLAY. If you play well in games, at practice, in camp or on film, you can get the attention of the coaches yourself and give them your direct contact information.

8 REASONS WHY PLAYERS MAY BEGIN TO BE RECRUITED
#5: Stood out as a great player at a college or university camp

By the end of your junior year (or better yet, your sophomore season), if you haven't been getting interest or offers from many schools, a great way to get on the map is by attending a university camp or two. It's also a great way to network with many other college and high school coaches who may also be able to help you with the process, along with getting the opportunity to see facilities and get a feel for being on a college campus.

Camps are an option to get your foot in the door but you will not directly be offered a scholarship on-site at the camp. NCAA rules prohibit against recruiting during camps, coaches are not able to "extend verbal or written offers of financial aid to any prospective student-athlete during their attendance at a camp or clinic." BUT, it is a good way for coaches to put a name with a face, to give them a chance to see your size, speed and skill in person and for you to get to know the campus, coaches and program better. Offer letters may be sent days or weeks down the road after you have made an impression on the coaches.

10 TIPS TO GO FROM CAMPER TO RECRUIT...

#1 – LET YOUR RECRUITING COACH KNOW THAT YOU ARE COMING AND WOULD LIKE AN EVALUATION: Call the camp office (the phone number should be on the brochure) a couple days before you go and tell the person who answers the telephone your name, position and high school. Ask which coach recruits your area or position. Write down their name and get their direct email address and phone number. Ask to be transferred to them—let them know or leave a voicemail telling them that you are coming to the camp in a couple days (don't call much sooner, they will forget), that you are emailing your highlight video right now and would like an evaluation, if possible, at the camp. Email them a link to your most recent highlights and include your name, jersey number, high school, position, graduation year, height, weight and contact information along with the camp date that you will be attending. When you arrive to check-in, ask a staff member if your recruiting coach is there and to point them out or see if they are able to introduce you to them. Tell them you are excited to be there say you would hope to get an evaluation and ask if they had a chance to look at the highlights that you sent them.

#2 – NETWORK WITH ALL OF YOUR COACHES: Get to know all of the coaches who are working the camp—not just the coaches from the school that is hosting the camp. Many camps, especially at major Division I programs, have several other college assistants working them, usually from smaller programs. Many coaches from other colleges may be there to network and recruit. They are usually connected to the coaches at the school that is hosting the camp, they may be old teammates, co-workers, friend of a friend or coaches who have previously met at a conference. There are also usually several area high school coaches that are working at the camp, and they may also have leads for you to other college coaches, from all different levels. During meals or down time simply pull them aside and ask them for ADVICE—let them do most of the talking. Tell them, "Coach, I really want to play on the next level, can you give me an evaluation, let me know what you think I need to work on in order to be recruited." This will open the door—some of your coaches may have no leads for you but MOST probably will. Even if you aren't someone THEY are interested in recruiting, most coaches are happy and willing to help and there is a chance that you may be a fit for a school where one of their friends coaches at. Some will be happy to make an introduction or call on your behalf, and you may get recruited from there. NETWORK with ALL of the coaches and simply ask for their advice—see where it takes you!

#3 – TEAM CAMPS: Team Camps are a great way to build chemistry with your team, network with coaches, get a chance to be on a college campus and to see how your team stacks up versus other teams in the area. Team Camps are also usually more affordable than Individual Camps and college coaches may but more emphasis on them as far as recruiting or making evaluations. Talk to your prep coaches or parents about the possibility of getting a group together and fundraising to go to a Team Camp or two, they are definitely great investments for your recruitment and your upcoming season!

#4 – GET A PART-TIME JOB: Camps can be expensive but if you believe you are worthy of being recruited and aren't getting the attention that you would like, they are a TREMENDOUS way to get your foot in the door to find out if there is any interest from a particular school or to network with several college coaches. Unfortunately, due to NCAA rules, no school is able to discount or offer need-based camp scholarships. But, never let money be an excuse—plan early and get a part-time job

NCAA RECRUIT TIPS: 7 STEPS TO A SCHOLARSHIP

or find out if your family is able to help you cover the cost of camp. Sessions usually run between $150-$300 for a few days worth of instruction. It is a really great investment! Camps could be something that you asked for as your birthday present, holiday present or something that you could possibly earn through chores or an allowance.

#5 – CAMP WITH YOUR HOMETOWN TEAM: If you aren't gaining much interest, start with the local universities that are near your home and try to get into their camp. Remember, one of the first questions a coach will ask you is, "Who have you been offered by." Even if it's not your dream school and you are just counting the minutes until you can move far, far away... it always will help you gain interest from other schools if you have a scholarship offer from the hometown team. See #2 – Not only will you be networking with the coaches from that school, you will likely be networking with coaches from other colleges who may have interest in recruiting you.

#6 – PRORATED CAMP FEES: Due to NCAA rules, schools are not able to discount camp rates or offer need-based scholarships... BUT, they are able to prorate camp fees. If you aren't able to afford the entire amount for a camp that lasts for several days, most schools do pro-rate their fees on a day-by-day or practice-by- practice basis. For example, if a camp is $300 for 5 days, you may be able to attend for one day for $60. You need to make the most of your time at this session—call before you go and let the recruiting coach know that you would like an evaluation if possible (send or bring your film highlights to the camp) and ask for advice from every coach that you are able to be around. Get there early and stay late, eat meals with staff and ask for ADVICE on getting your foot in the door to be recruited. Squeeze as much networking and learning into the day as possible! Learn or ask the coaches for some position-specific drills that you may be able to do on your own to improve.

#7 – COMPETITIVE OR ELITE CAMPS: Many major universities host smaller, more competitive camps that they like to emphasize to the players who they are evaluating or currently recruiting. Due to NCAA rules, camps must be "open to any and all entrants, limited only by number, age, grade level and or gender," so any player who would like to attend (within this limitations) may do so. Even if you haven't been personally invited by the coaches like some of the other players, you are able to attend and can still get your foot in the door with the coaches. A few players get recognized and begin to get recruited this way, so don't worry if you weren't invited or recruited to come like some of the other players. Call each program that you are interested in and ask them if they plan on hosting a Senior Camp, Elite Camp or Competitive Camp for recruits. Sometimes information isn't advertised until a couple weeks before the camp, so continue to check in every month during the summer to find out if they are hosting such an event.

#8 – BEST WAY TO GET COACHES ATTENTION WHILE YOU ARE THERE: Outside of elite skill, size and speed, coaches are always looking for players who are fundamentally solid and who know how to do the dirty work—the acts that help win games that most players don't necessarily want to do or the plays that don't necessary get the media or fan glory. Don't go into the camp trying to make a big ESPN-Top 10 worthy play... go into the camp trying to be the most fundamentally sound and most physical player of the camp. Coaches LOVE players who hustle—players who make the textbook tackle and know how to finish; players who dive for balls, play defense and who can be a difference-maker on the boards; players who aren't just trying to always be flashy but who are always trying to make EACH play that comes their way. Don't focus on making that ONE extraordinary play... focus on making every play count. Coaches aren't looking for flash—they are looking for fundamentals. Want some extra credit? Go out to the field 10-15 minutes early and if the drills are set up (and there are coaches or trainers on the field) get in some extra work, ask for position-specific drills that you can do on your own at home!

#9 – STAY OFF YOUR FEET: If you are really trying to get noticed at the camp, treat it as many college and pro players do—like pre-season training camp. Stay hydrated, eat well and stay off your feet! If you are attending an overnight camp, instead of running around the dorms like a 6-year-old and cannonballing into the pool, get to bed early and give your body some rest so that you will be ready for the next practice. During the season, many college coaches are constantly reminding their players: "STAY OFF YOUR FEET!" Stay hydrated while at practice and make sure to drink plenty of water or sports drinks at all of your meals. Avoid the pizza, junk food and fried foods at the dining hall and stick to the leaner meats, healthy carbs, fruits and vegetables. If possible, bring some extra drinks and bananas to your room to be able to rehydrate during the night. You don't want to lose valuable practice time because of cramps or dehydration!

#10 – TEMPORARY INSURANCE: Most camps will require campers to show proof of insurance—if you aren't covered but still want to participate in the camp, check into temporary policies that usually are very affordable that can give you 30-days of coverage.

WHAT SUCCESSFUL PLAYERS KNOW: THERE IS ENOUGH SHINE FOR EVERYONE. QUIT WORRYING ABOUT TEAMMATES STEALING THE SPOTLIGHT, THERE IS PLENTY TO GO AROUND!

Most coaches that I've worked for would at least give you a look at camp if you've gone out of your way to make that initial contact with them and to follow-up at check-in. Coaches naturally enjoy helping players and most will be happy to give you a 5-10 minute evaluation, even if you aren't a player who they will likely recruit.

Have your highlights available to bring up on your smartphone or tablet on the spot and have a copy of your Student-Athlete Resume in hand. Or bring a copy of your game DVD or highlights to leave with the coaches. Take advantage of the few one-on-one moments you may be able to squeeze in!

They key to making the most of this process is accepting what the coach tells you! Do not get discouraged! Remember—go into camp with an open mind, relaxed heart and good attitude. Remember— when you put pressure on yourself is when you make errors that you wouldn't normally make, so be sure to just RELAX and HAVE FUN! Most coaches truly enjoy helping you! Make this a positive experience for your recruitment, not a negative one. You should take their evaluations and accept them—they are professionals and have evaluated players on a near daily basis for years. They know EXACTLY what they're looking for in a recruit for their system, style of play and program. You can't argue your way into a scholarship offer—instead, simply listen to their PRICELESS feedback!

Use this time to be productive—get the most for your money! You may only get two minutes of their time (if that) so understand that coaches will be honest and direct with you. Listen to what they have to say. If they recommend that you try smaller programs—do so! If they say they have a buddy who coaches at another school down the road, get their contact info and name and follow-through. It's a foot in the door that you didn't have yesterday!

Working to raise the money to pay for camp will be just another test of your mental toughness, a toughness that will be challenged daily whether you play Division III or develop into an All-Pro player. All champions have mastered the art of 'finding a way'—and sometimes that starts with finding a way to work your way to camp!

8 REASONS WHY PLAYERS MAY BEGIN TO BE RECRUITED
#6: Sent a highlight video to the coaches and they were impressed

In most sports, another quick way to get on a school's radar is by sending in a copy of your highlight video. Remember, the only way a coach can tell if you are worthy of a scholarship offer is by seeing you play or compete—either in person or on video! If schools haven't come to YOU and if you can't get to their campus for camp, the only other legit way to get their attention, in most sports, is by sending your highlight video by mail or email.

Some high school coaches can help you put together your highlights or there are services that can also assist you. Either way, it is a step that can greatly help you in the recruiting process.

FOLLOWING UP AFTER A COLLEGE COACH TOLD YOU TO GIVE THEM A CALL OR SEND YOUR VIDEO

Coaches normally mean what they say, and say what they mean. If a coach gives you their contact info and tells you to call them—call them, and call them soon! Often I would get calls from high school seniors or their parents, telling me they met coaches years or months ago—and are calling to see if any scholarships are still available. Usually, no! If a coach tells you to contact them—especially if you aren't getting much other interest—and gives you their cell or office number, they're interested on some level and you can't just expect them to chase you around if you are also somewhat interested. Call to check in, send them your highlights or game video. Don't let the introduction you made go stale without getting an evaluation of your play! If you follow-up months or years later (or even weeks later, in some cases) those scholarship dollars are gone!

15 TIPS FOR PUTTING TOGETHER YOUR HIGHLIGHT VIDEOS

#1: Send highlights from varsity games only

#2: Send recent highlights, games within the last year (unless you sat out due to injury)

#3: Be sure to note your jersey number and jersey color (white/dark) so that coaches can identify you quickly

#4: If possible, send highlights that show you specifically

#5: Include 15-30 plays from multiple games

#6: Keep highlights between 2-5 minutes

#7: If possible, also send 2-3 full or half games. Coaches may request full games in order to evaluate further after you get their attention through highlights.

#8: Show all position-specific skills, you want to show you are a well-rounded player

#9: No music is necessary

#10: No fancy cover is necessary

#11: Be sure to send your Student-Athlete Resume with your highlights (mail or email)

#12: Don't email to generic email accounts, contact the school to get the direct email address of the coach who recruits your area or position

#13: You must follow-up after a week for feedback

#14: If you aren't getting much of a response, contact the team and ask for a grad assistant or Director of Operations or ask to speak with someone who works in recruiting

#15: If you can't find a coach's email address, it never hurts to hit them up on social media and tweet or Facebook your highlight links to them, publicly or privately.

If you haven't been contacted by the end of your junior season, it's time to put together you highlights immediately after the season and begin to send them out to coaches at schools that you are interested in, and to several (or all!) schools within the state. And for seniors, if you are starting the process late, get those highlights on YouTube or Hudl and start sending them out—NOW!

Once you have your highlights finished, you can send your video via email, social media or by mailing a hard copy. Again—your first job is to get the name of the specific coach who recruits your city or position. Get their direct email address and direct phone number. Once you make your list of coaches and get their DIRECT contact info, send it to their attention along with your Student-Athlete Resume and be sure to follow-up within a week or two!

HIGHLIGHTS VS. FULL GAME VIDEO

Which do coaches prefer? Have them both ready and included in what you mail/email to coaches, if possible.

Coaches get tons of emails with YouTube/Hudl links and hard copies of DVDs from players and have a limited amount of time to go through unsolicited videos. Remember, they are also viewing or requesting film on players they have already heard about and investing more time with those potential recruits who they've already heard about from trusted sources. The first hurdle will be to get someone to actually watch it.

When coaches sit down to watch unsolicited films they can often tell within a 20-30 seconds if you have the size and speed to be successful within their program. If they like what they see from those initial evaluations, they will move on to your game film links or request them from you or your coach. It's great to send both if available so they have everything right there and can look at in one setting, make the most of your opportunity.

If coaches like what they see on your videos, they will pick up the phone and call your coach or rival coaches in the area. They may do more research, make plans to add you to their recruiting watch list or make plans to come out to see you in person. Getting the right people to watch your videos can be the first step to opening the door to scholarship offers.

*WHEN YOU DON'T BELIEVE
THAT YOUR DREAMS
CAN ACTUALLY COME TRUE,
YOU STOP TRYING!
YOU ARE DEFEATED
BEFORE YOU HAVE EVEN STARTED!*

@1001RecruitTips

HOW TO GET THE COACH'S CONTACT INFORMATION AND HOW TO GET AN EVALUATION OF YOUR HIGHLIGHT VIDEO

- Find the official athletic department website. Google it!

- Most official university athletic websites have a 'Department Directory' or a 'Staff Directory' link. Find the phone number for the Athletic Department switchboard or the direct number for you specific sport. Some schools list direct phone numbers and emails for assistant coaches on their website, others may not and post a generic number for everyone.

- Call the office of your specific team—either directly or call the main athletic department switchboard and ask to be transferred to that specific sport ("Can I please be transferred to the lacrosse office?")

- Introduce yourself and say, "Hi, I am Johnny Recruit and I'm from Nashville, TN and I'm a linebacker at Nashville North Prep. I wanted to send my info to the coach who recruits my area. Could you tell me who that is?"

- Write down the coaches' name.

- Ask for their mailing address, direct phone number and email address. Write everything down.

SCHOOL	ATHLETIC DEPT RECEPTION PHONE #	RECRUITING COACH FOR YOUR HOMETOWN OR POSITION	RECRUITING COACHES DIRECT PHONE #	RECRUITING COACHES MAILING ADDRESS	RECRUITING COACHES DIRECT EMAIL	NOTES

- Ask to be transferred to that coach.

- If it goes to voicemail: leave your name, grad year, school name and position. Tell them that you are going to email or mail a copy of your highlight film to them today, say "Coach I was really interested in your program and wanted to know if you could check out my video and give me some feedback." Tell them you will give them a call in a couple days to follow-up. Keep it short, their voicemail may cut you off.

- If the coach answers, give them the same information, "Hi Coach, this is Johnny Recruit and I'm a junior from Nashville, TN and I'm a linebacker at Nashville North Prep. I'm sending you my highlight video today and was wondering if you'd be able to take a look at it and let me know what you think. I'm really interested in your program." The conversation will go from there—remember, tell them that you will FOLLOW-UP in a couple days.

NCAA RECRUIT TIPS: 7 STEPS TO A SCHOLARSHIP

- Send your highlight video via mail or email along with your Student-Athlete Resume that includes your name, position, jersey number, height, weight, speed, contact information, high school, travel team information, coaches contact information and grades.

- In two or three days (no longer than that) follow-up with the coach that you sent the information to. "Coach, this is Johnny Recruit from Nashville North Prep, I spoke to you on Wednesday and was wondering if you had the chance to take a look at my video." If you get their voicemail again, leave the same message. Tell them that you will call back in a few days.

- If after three phone calls you still aren't able to get in contact with the coach, call back the main office and ask if a grad assistant or Director of Operations is available. Start the introduction again from the beginning, get their name, direct email address and phone number. Send your highlight video to them. Follow-up in a few days.

- If you are a junior or YOUNGER and still aren't able to get feedback, wait a few weeks. Or, try back again in the off-season when the coach may have a little more time. If you are a senior, ask one of your prep coaches if they can give them a call to see if they are able to get an evaluation.

Understand that most coaches receive multiple unsolicited emails each day, up to 10 or more a day from players and coaches who reach out on their own! These emails sometimes get lost in the masses of messages in their inbox, especially if they don't recognize your name. Between staff meetings, other more urgent emails from known contacts, practice, issues with current players, workouts, film review and priority recruiting calls, these unsolicited emails can get lost in the shuffle.

Coaches regularly request videos of high school players on their watch lists, particularly in football. At most FBS schools, if a football coach didn't request the film, they're normally not going to set aside the time to watch it. They simply don't have the time, but don't let this be a dead end for you!

It's CRITICAL that you take the extra step to follow-up with coaches. Many prep players assume their video was viewed and rejected and never follow-up when truthfully, most unsolicited videos or emails don't always get watched right away. But if you follow-up on the phone, there is a decent chance that they'll watch it or have someone on staff take a look at it.

Within some programs, a grad assistant or intern is designated to review videos that are received from players that were not requested, players coaches may know nothing about. If the grad assistant or intern sees something in you, they'll bring it to the recruiting coach to watch it, and if they see something they need, they'll begin to send you mail, call you, come check you out in person or possibly show your video to the head coach as a potential scholarship player. These grad assistants or interns are looking to climb their way up in the office ranks and one great way of doing this is by finding future playmakers for their coaches to recruit. Remember, assistant coaches are ALWAYS looking for a diamond in the rough, and if the intern finds that next big one it could mean a promotion for them down the road.

Coaches will NEVER come out to see you play if they haven't seen you on video first or heard really great things about you from a trusted source. You must give them a reason to come check you out!

If your highlights get forwarded on to the recruiting coach and they like you, they'll add you to their watch list and likely make plans to come see you play in person. Simple as that.

Too many players would get transferred to my office who couldn't remember the name of the coach that they'd spoken to a week earlier and it gives off an unprofessional impression. It makes you look like you don't really care and know nothing about the program. When you call, always take notes, you better be sure that the coaches are on the other line!

SACRIFICE = SUCCESS

As an operations assistant, there were times I could barely get two minutes in to ask my questions—so don't be offended that a coach hasn't spent 10 minutes chasing down your video and watching it. Sorry to keep harping on this but.. they just truly don't have the time. They could strictly watch unsolicited videos all day and still never finish!

Another good thing to remember is that most coaching staffs have a regular routine with their schedule, especially during the season or during organized off- season workouts. In football, every Monday has the same schedule, every Tuesday has the same schedule, etc. Other sports that play multiple games per week have a similar daily routine: morning staff meeting, lunch/exercise break, time to return phone calls, player meetings or film sessions, practice, meetings. Between 11am-2pm is probably the best time to reach coaches in their office, they might not be there the whole time but they should be there at some time during that window, unless it's a gameday!

In most cases, a coach or staff person will take a look at it if they know you're going to call back. They have to prioritize what is urgent in their world first, and that usually involves projects for the head coach, preparing for practice, returning phone calls or an issue with a current player or top recruit.

Once a coach has watched your video and you are able to get them on the phone or to return an email – the next step is to take their evaluation. In some cases, this may be a quick rejection!

Almost every coach will give you an honest but direct evaluation of your video. Again, they do this for a living, and probably have been evaluating

NCAA RECRUIT TIPS: 7 STEPS TO A SCHOLARSHIP

talent for 10 to 20 years. They know what type of player will fit their system and which will be able to compete and be successful in their conference. They don't always sugarcoat it, so again—don't get defensive, make the most of this opportunity!

I don't know ONE coach who likes telling a prep player that they aren't good enough for their team. IT'S THE HARDEST PART OF THEIR JOB. But... they will be direct with you because it hurts both of you in the long run if they sugarcoat it and lead you on. They don't have the time to spend with you if you keep calling back and YOU need to figure out the next school and coach to contact in order to get on the right path.

But, this is where you can make the most of your opportunity. Ask them ONE more question—"Coach, would you suggest any teams or coaches that are looking for a player like me?"

Some coaches may say no and hang up, but there is a small chance they'll have some leads for you. Again, coaches know other coaches everywhere—so they may have a few schools that you could be a fit for. In some cases, they may even make a call or two or forward your email and highlights for you if they have a relationship with coaches at those other schools—they're usually an old college teammate or former co-worker. They're helping out their buddy and doing their good deed for the day.

If you go into this process and respect the fact that coaches and their support staff are very busy, you can sometimes get some good (and free) advice. The toughest part is actually getting to the right person and being persistent without being annoying! Don't call every day, don't call every week. Don't talk too much, don't tell them your life story. Don't make excuses why nobody has discovered you yet or get defensive or forceful. Don't bother the coach during the season when their schedule is overloaded.

DO be patient! DO stay positive!

Keep it short and simple, "Coach, can you take a quick look at my video and let me know what you think."

IF YOU NEED AN EDGE, SEPARATE YOURSELF BY DOING THE JOBS NOBODY ELSE WANTS. LEARNING HOW TO SUCCEED AT THE DIRTY WORK WILL GET YOU MOVED UP THE DEPTH CHART.

8 REASONS WHY PLAYERS MAY BEGIN TO BE RECRUITED
#7: *Were offered by a rival or comparable school within the conference or region*

Another common reason why coaches may look into your abilities is if a rival, conference or comparable school offers you a scholarship. It is very common to hear a head coach go into an assistant coach's office and say, "Hey, the big kid from St. Louis just got offered by School XYZ, what did you think of him?"

Coaches are always keeping an eye on the competition and they also expect their assistant coaches to know about EVERY POSSIBLE prospect in their assigned geographic region or position. They will want to know why that assistant coach didn't think they were worthy of recruitment or an offer... or they will put that assistant coach into action to get a copy of your film in order to evaluate you for themselves.

ATHLETIC DEPARTMENTS HAVE ACADEMIC ADVISORS WHO PROJECT HOW YOU WILL DO AS A STUDENT AND IF YOU ARE WORTH THE TIME TO RECRUIT. CAN YOU SUCCEED ACADEMICALLY IS DISCUSSED!

If you are offered by a school, you will likely get looks from their rivals or schools within the conference to see if you are someone they should be offering too.

When you begin approaching coaches on your own, one of the first questions they will ask you is, "Who have you been offered by?" Your answer will give them a starting point in their research, so even if it's a less competitive school than you may be interested in, it does give other coaches an idea of your talent.

Never lie about what schools have offered you! Coaches quickly do their research and will find out and possibly eliminate you. There is nothing wrong with saying, "I have no offers yet," it doesn't necessarily mean you aren't talented, it only means you haven't been discovered yet.

8 REASONS WHY PLAYERS MAY BEGIN TO BE RECRUITED
#8: *Political Ties (Friend of top recruit, family member of influential person within the University or Athletic Department)*

College coaches are pitched about prospective prospects by some powerful people within the University and Athletic Department: long-time donors, University Board of Trustees members, former players, professional players, CEOs, celebrities—and may spend some time with these prospects above and beyond what they may have spent if there were no political ties. Or, when top prospects are looking at schools with their best friend, wanting to play college sports together, they may show more interest in the best friend than they normally would have shown without that tie.

NCAA RECRUIT TIPS: 7 STEPS TO A SCHOLARSHIP

This isn't a factor that you should bank on or work to make happen for yourself but I am throwing it in there because there ARE players who earn scholarship offers or opportunities to walk on to a team because of their long-term relationships with top prospects or influential people tied to the University, Athletic Department or Coach.

Many programs carry one or two players on their roster who are relatives of major boosters, donors or influential people with the university or athletic department, most of them as walk-ons. A coaching staff may begin to send mail and notecards to these prep players but may not be reserving a scholarship, rather simply saving them a spot as a priority walk-on.

When an elite player wants to play with their best friend (who may not be near as talented) there are schools that will make that offer, sacrificing that spot from a more worthy player. They may want to do anything to get an edge in the recruitment or want that elite player to feel their most comfortable with their best friend on the roster with them. Some schools are willing to take the hit, others may not be.

IF YOU ARE TRULY TRYING YOUR HARDEST, NEVER LOSE FAITH IN YOURSELF. JUST BECAUSE THE SHINE AND CROWDS AREN'T THERE (YET), THAT DOESN'T MEAN YOU AREN'T IMPROVING!

Throughout my career I have worked with coaches who have actively recruited and offered players who were very talented, who just happened to be related to influential people or celebrities. Their connections may have nothing to do with why a player is recruited, it could 100% based on their talent.

But, business in any industry still revolves around this type of preferential treatment... that will never change. In the business of big money college athletics, these walk-on positions are sometimes given to those with influence around the program or university.

If the athletes have legitimate talent and are children of high-profile athletes or CEOs, they may get a few more national scholarships than they normally would, simply for the exposure or buzz it may bring to the program... or for the potential to gain a new financial supporter. A few may be given the chance but many have actually earned it.

Particularly for potential walk-ons, it's important to understand that many of these positions are already spoken for, so becoming a walk-on may not be as easy as you think.

Politics will play their way onto any team and there isn't much you can do about it! Again, it's about finding a school who is excited to have a player like you!

INTEREST VS. SCHOLARSHIP OFFERS
All these emails, letters, cards, phone calls and Unofficial Visits won't mean much at the end of the day, unless they lead to scholarship offers, right?

Coaches put a ton of time into evaluations. They watch several games, try to see you play in person, contact several coaches and sources in the area to find out more about you as a person AND athlete. It's a process, and they can keep their eyes on you for months before deciding to offer a scholarship.

"Interest" means they've seen or heard something about you from a trusted source, and have added you to their "Watch List." Coaches are gathering info from several sources, combines and camps. They cast a huge net with each recruiting class (and position group within each class), to identify the best possible prospects for their system, university and team.

Beyond athletic ability, coaches are looking at leadership, morals, toughness and other intangibles. Can you become really great at a certain skill that can help lead to wins? Can you become a better blocker, defender, rebounder or help by creating turnovers? Sure, coaches are looking for scorers, but they're also looking for other difference-makers that can help them win. Can you develop better skills, speed, strength and a specific "difference-maker" ability? Look at the pros at your position—the elite players are usually masters of one specific skill.

It's difficult to be patient, but you have to understand it's an in-depth process with most head coaches wanting input from several of the assistant coaches before making offer decisions.

GETTING THE FIRST SCHOLARSHIP OFFER, ALWAYS THE TOUGHEST!
The goal of each recruiting cycle for each coaching staff is to sign the best player possible to each scholarship. Many staffs don't rush the process, they'd rather get it RIGHT than simply make it QUICK.

Understand—it's a PROCESS.

I've worked with players who earned offers days or weeks before Signing Day. I've worked with coaches who don't use all of their scholarships until they are 100% confident in a player they decide to offer, they don't just use every spot until they are sold on a specific player who can help their team.

In certain situations, a coach doesn't want to offer a player they are sure will commit until they are 100% sold on that player and confident they will be admitted into school and be eligible through the NCAA Eligibility Center—so many players have had to wait weeks or months in order to have a decision from a coaching staff.

NCAA RECRUIT TIPS: 7 STEPS TO A SCHOLARSHIP

Remember—you just need to find that one coaching staff who believes in you and you must be patient with the process!

On the bright side, after you get that first scholarship offer it can be easier to attract attention or get your foot in the door with other programs!

YOU MUST NOT ONLY BE PATIENT IN WAITING FOR YOUR OPPORTUNITY, YOU MUST BE PATIENT IN YOUR IMPROVEMENTS. GREATNESS OCCURS OVER TIME WITH CONSISTENT EFFORT!

ACTION STEPS: GETTING STARTED & GETTING NOTICED

- **GET VIDEO TOGETHER:** THIS IS MOST LIKELY THE MOST IMPORTANT STEP YOU CAN TAKE TO HELP GET MORE EXPOSURE, ONCE YOU HAVE SOME VARSITY PLAYING TIME UNDER YOUR BELT! IT DOESN'T NECESSARILY MATTER WHICH METHOD YOU USE (YOUTUBE, HUDL, ETC.), WHAT MATTERS IS THAT YOU GET SOME VIDEO TOGETHER USING OUR 15 TIPS (PAGE 50).

- **PUT TOGETHER YOUR STUDENT-ATHLETE RESUME:** CONSIDER THE PROCESS LIKE A JOB INTERVIEW! COACHES SKIM THROUGH HUNDREDS OF "APPLICANTS" A WEEK! PUT ALL OF YOUR IMPORTANT ACADEMIC, ATHLETIC AND CONTACT INFORMATION IN A QUICK AND EASY-TO-READ FORMAT SO COACHES CAN QUICKLY GET A PICTURE OF YOUR BACKGROUND WHILE WATCHING YOUR FILM, WITH YOUR CONTACT INFO AT THEIR FINGERTIPS! SEE PAGE 29 FOR EXAMPLES.

- **DEVELOP A LIST OF SCHOOLS THAT YOU ARE INTERESTED IN OR OPEN TO CONSIDERING:** DEVELOP YOUR TARGET LIST AND ALSO BE SURE TO INCLUDE PLENTY OF REALISTIC SCHOOLS AND PROGRAMS. START WITH AT LEAST 10 POTENTIAL PROGRAMS THAT YOU WANT TO BEGIN REACHING OUT TO.

- **DEVELOP A LOCAL LIST OF UNIVERSITIES:** TO HELP GET THE PROCESS GOING, ALSO BE SURE TO INCLUDE SEVERAL LOCAL SCHOOLS THAT ARE LOCATED WITHIN 2-4 HOURS FROM YOUR HOME (EVEN IF YOU PREFER TO GO AWAY FURTHER TO SCHOOL). GENERATING LOCAL INTEREST CAN HELP YOU DOWN THE ROAD.

- **8 WAYS PLAYERS GET NOTICED – YOUR STRATEGY:** REVIEW THE 8 WAYS (PAGE 34) AND PLAN YOUR STRATEGY BASED ON WHAT'S REALISTIC FOR YOU AND YOUR FAMILY. NOT EVERYONE CAN TRAVEL FROM CAMP TO CAMP OR PLAY ON TRAVEL TEAMS, BUT THERE IS ZERO EXCUSE OF WHY YOU CAN'T GET NOTICED BECAUSE THERE ARE SEVERAL DIFFERENT OPPORTUNITIES TO GET YOUR NAME OUT THERE! TRY TO START WITH AT LEAST 2-3 WAYS!

  - SCOUTING SERVICES
  - CAMPS
  - COMBINES
  - HIGHLIGHT VIDEO
  - GAMES & TOURNEYS
  - OFFERED BY RIVAL
  - RECOMMENDED BY PREP COACH

- **UNDERSTAND THAT EYES ARE EVERYWHERE:** CARRY YOURSELF AS IF A COLLEGE COACH IS IN YOUR PRESENCE, AT ALL TIMES. IT'S A FACT THAT COLLEGE COACHES ARE GETTING RECOMMENDATIONS, REFERRALS AND EVALUATIONS FROM PEOPLE EVERYWHERE. EVEN IF A COLLEGE COACH ISN'T SHOWING UP AT YOUR GAMES QUITE YET, UNDERSTAND THAT SOMEONE THEY TRUST MAY BE GIVING THEM FEEDBACK ABOUT RECRUIT-WORTHY PLAYERS IN THE AREA! GIVE PEOPLE A REASON TO RECOMMEND YOU WHEN COLLEGE COACHES COME CALLING IN YOUR REGION!

STEP #3
UNDERSTAND HOW COACHES EVALUATE PLAYERS & BUILD THEIR SIGNING CLASS

"Success is to be measured not so much by position that one has reached as by the obstacles which he has overcome."
-BOOKER T. WASHINGTON

"ACTION is the foundational key to all success."
-PABLO PICASSO

"Every leader must establish a list of priorities-- and then put first things FIRST."
-JOHN C. MAXWELL

INSIDE THE COACHES' OFFICE: HOW COACHES ASSIGN RECRUITING RESPONSIBILITIES

Nearly every program splits recruiting responsibilities between the staff, primarily by geographic region or by position. Each staff may designate an assistant coach or staff member as the coordinator but normally each assistant coach has an equal responsibility to sign players. One of your first assignments is to find out which coach is responsible for recruiting your area or position at each school that you are interested in.

Many players and parents make the mistake of demanding or waiting to speak to the head coach first, you'll get through MUCH quicker by asking for the coach who scouts your area or position.

Unless you are a McDonald's All-American or Gatorade Player of the Year, the head coach probably won't be calling you back!

Once you can get your video and info to the coach who recruits your area or position (more about this later) and they are impressed and are interested in recruiting you or offering you, they will take your information to the head coach and your recruitment will go from there. Assistant coaches do their research on you before alerting the head coach about you as a potential recruit, that's why it's so critical that you start with them first! In most cases, even if you are able to meet or speak with the head coach, they'll likely forward you or your information to the appropriate assistant coach without spending much personal time on it—this is the chain of command within most teams.

GREAT PLAYERS AREN'T AFRAID OF COMPETITION... PERIOD. ANYONE, ANYWHERE. ANYTIME...

Many programs split up the home state, giving each assistant coach an assigned area to monitor and build relationships in. Most schools make it a priority to keep "the best players in the state at home," making sure each of the assistant coaches play a role in identifying ALL potential recruits in the state and building relationships with prep coaches and programs at home. Each assistant is often assigned a handful of counties to become an expert in within the state.

In most cases, college coaches still put a lot of attention to in-state high schools even if they currently have no prospects. They are building long-term relationships for the future so that once the school has a great player they will already have close relationships with the coaching staff. They're never just building for that season, they're building for the future.

Major metropolitan areas are usually assigned after that—Atlanta, DC/Baltimore, Dallas, Houston, Chicago, Los Angeles. Key states and regions are assigned from there— Florida, California, Texas, Northeast, Midwest, West Coast and so on. Staffs cover the map—usually including an

NCAA RECRUIT TIPS: 7 STEPS TO A SCHOLARSHIP

international contact—so your first priority is identifying these assistant coaches at the schools that you are interested in who are responsible for recruiting your AREA or POSITION.

For example, when an SEC head football coach hires his assistants, they all need strong Florida, Georgia and Alabama ties. They will also need a mix of coaches with ties to the Northeast, East Coast, Midwest, Texas and West Coast. Same thing for West Coast teams, they have assistant coaches with ties across California, Washington and Oregon as well as a mix of staff that has strong ties to the Midwest, Northeast and the South. Each school has a regional focus in recruiting, and each program varies with the level of emphasis that they put on recruiting at a national level, usually dependent on their budget.

Coaches are normally assigned specific geographic regions because it's an area they grew up in, went to college in, have worked in before or have previous ties to. It's also helpful for coaches to have personal ties to those regions: parents of recruits (and their extended families) oftentimes have mutual friends with college coaches which helps in building relationships during the process! It always helps in building relationships if coaches are a friend of a cousin, brother, mother and those ties can go back decades. Coaches want parents and players to feel a built-in familiarity with them, and that has a lot to do with long-term personal relationships. Good or bad, they have a 'track record' in the area.

Most head coaches will say that their priority is to recruit and keep the best in-state players at home, but all major FBS programs will recruit nationally for the best talent possible. Smaller schools may focus more regionally since they have smaller budgets and less media coverage. Smaller schools may focus on prospects within driving distance instead of constantly flying coaches across the country to market their program or regularly flying recruits in on expensive flights.

Long term, established relationships that NCAA coaches have with prep programs are often the reason that many assistants are actually hired. They are able to provide an immediate pipeline to a targeted area, the staff won't have to start from scratch when getting to know high school and AAU coaches in the area. Many coaches have built their careers off the foundation of having a strong history of signing players (and taking care of them while they are coaching them) from certain regions. I've worked with many whose strengths were in their recruiting connections—to Maryland, Washington, DC, Atlanta, Orlando, New York City, Miami and New Jersey.

Once you can identify your recruiting coaches at the schools that you are interested in, get on their radar by sending your highlight video and Student-Athlete Resume. That is the only true way to get your foot in the door and be taken serious!

HOW THE COACHING STAFF RANKS PLAYERS

Most staffs have a ranking system within their prospect database, a way to rate recruits by their ability or by the level of attention that they want to give them in terms of mail (form letters or hand-written notes), email, calls and what events they get invited to.

Common groups include:
- Players who are being actively recruited (juniors and seniors)
- Top priorities to get a commitment from next (wish list of top recruits)
- Current commitments (recruiting doesn't end even after a player commits)
- Plan B Players (backup plans or players who may be out-of-reach)
- Top Underclassmen who are too young to be contacted
- Players who were evaluated earlier and labeled as 'not talented enough at this time'
- Players who coaches were previously interested in who committed to other schools

Most commonly, each assistant coach has a top list of players that they are 'actively recruiting.' Depending on what time of year it is and where they are in the recruiting cycle, this is the list of prospects that they will regularly call, visit, do research on and try to get to campus for an unofficial or official visit. 'Actively recruiting' is the key phrase, and this group includes players who have already committed to their school, players who have already been offered a scholarship or players who are on the verge of getting an offer.

Some coaches like to create sub-lists of these top players that they are actively recruiting. This is the group they've already gotten commitments from or players who are on the top of their wish list— the best of the best.

Beyond these two groups, there is often a B-list of players. These are prospects who could potentially be backup offers if the first, second, third or fourth choices don't work out. These prospects usually receive some mail, emails and who may get an invite to junior days, scrimmages or games. This list may also include players who coaches may think are unattainable, players who are long-shots that they may still check in with or mail information to, just hoping for a chance to get their foot in the door.

Beyond those lists, coaches normally keep lists of top underclassmen (who are too young to contact), players that have committed to other schools and prospects that they determined are currently not talented enough for their program. Coaches keep extra files, even if a player is cut from their watch list, since the statuses of players often changes— players decommit, get better, have a growth spurt or re-classify grades. I've seen many players cut from our 'actively recruiting' list who re-surfaced months later and were added back on and ended up signing scholarships.

In some cases, primarily in football, coaches from other schools may continue to recruit you even if you have committed publicly to another school. Verbal commitments in football aren't always final, so it's common for rival coaches to continue to keep calling, visiting and marketing. If you ever find yourself in this situation and are overwhelmed, you CAN tell these other coaches that you are done with the process and to go ahead and drop you from their list—many will back off after that.

How you are ranked within their database determines how much mail you receive, what kind of mail you receive, which coaches are coming to see you, who's calling you, and what games/events you are invited to. Everybody isn't treated the same but it's important to understand where you may fit in within the staffs' rankings. Are you a priority to them or are they recruiting several players ahead of you at your position? You need to understand that it's important to keep your options open!

HOW COACHES BUILD THEIR 'WATCH LISTS'

Coaches work off a list of players that they are recruiting, let's call it their 'watch list.' They are constantly adding and subtracting names from their personal list and begin to build one as a staff for each graduating class as early as your freshman year. Separate lists by each group are constantly growing and being edited: seniors, juniors, sophomores, freshman, Junior College players and International athletes. Just because they can't contact you as a freshman or sophomore, that doesn't mean that they aren't already getting organized and doing their research on your class!

Schools may pay thousands of dollars for the databases that they use to help keep everyone organized and connected. Databases are updated daily, players are added and internal rankings are always changing! Many have email features and are able to keep track of more information than you'd ever want to know about.

There are nine main reasons why a coach may begin recruiting you (and add you to the database) that we will be discussing shortly. Once they add you to their watch list and you are a junior or senior (permissible for them to contact by NCAA rules) they may begin to send you mail, request your highlight video and communicate with you until they decide to make the trip out to come see you play in person and evaluate you for themselves.

There is a scramble in the time from when college coaches add you to their watch list... to getting a chance to personally evaluate you for themselves... to getting a feel for your intangibles (attitude, work ethic, academics, family issues), your raw athletic talent and your interest level in their program. Each coaches' watch list of juniors and seniors changes weekly or even daily.

Again, lists for each recruiting class are generated as early as your freshman year. Coaches are constantly adding freshman and sophomores to their database based off observations from games, practices and tournaments as well as from reports produced by regional scouting services that they subscribe to. Coaches are building this list, sending questionnaires to you and researching your contact information so that they will be prepared to contact you once they are legally able to according to NCAA rules.

Don't think that coaches sit around waiting for your junior or senior year to start planning on who they will recruit. Know that college coaches are always three steps ahead in their research and evaluations, and they're always trying to discover the best players in the area before every other college does, and build those relationships with prospects' coaches and high schools first.

These watch lists are the first point of reference that coaches use when planning their travel schedules to evaluate talent during evaluation and contact periods. Coaches take their base watch lists out on the road at the beginning of each evaluation period and will add and subtract recruits based on their in-person evaluations.

> **THERE COMES A TIME WHEN YOU MUST PUT YOUR DREAMS AND GOALS INTO ACTION. NO SUCCESS WILL COME OF JUST DREAMS AND GOALS, SUCCESS COMES AFTER YOU TAKE ACTION ON THOSE DREAMS AND GOALS.**

For example, each assistant coach may have a list of 25-30 top players on their watch list (who are getting mail and calls) and they are still trying to evaluate another 20 potential players. After those in-person evaluations, they will likely drop five to ten top players but come back with 10 new names to add.

Again, even if you are on a national or state Top 100 list, that doesn't mean that every coach will think you are a good fit for their system and program. And just because you aren't on any Top 100 lists, it doesn't mean that coaches won't be watching and won't notice you—they are specifically at these events to find the best talent, size and speed. Coaches can sense talent pretty quickly and to them, it doesn't matter if you are a 5-star player or an unranked player. If they like your skills—they will recruit you... simple as that!

Watch lists change daily. You can be dropped with no explanation, at any time, for circumstances you can't always control. On the flip side, know that you can also show up on any coach's' radar overnight, so keep working hard and remain positive!

WHAT'S MORE IMPORTANT - SIZE VS. SKILL?

The main factors coaches are evaluating are position-specific skills, size, strength and speed. Most players may not be great at all four, but being exceptional with any of those qualities can help you get on the map or get the recruiting conversations going.

Never let someone tell you that you are "too small" or "too slow" to play college sports—if you have the talent, you can work your way to scholarship offers somewhere. Some coaching staffs sit down and determine physical sizes they are looking for at each position and may not make many exceptions, other staffs are more flexible if the skills outweigh the size issues.

Not every school may be willing to take a look if you are undersized or "slow" for your position—but you just need to find that one coaching staff who believes in you.

I have worked with players who may have had great measurable who lacked position skills. Since many coaches feel they can teach position skills, they may recruit players who already have the great size and speed—it just depends on how that staff evaluates players for scholarships.

Great skill, toughness and a high sport IQ can overcome a lack of size or speed.

Continue to develop great fundamentals of your position and set goals to improve your measurables. You may not be able to control your height but there are ways to improve your skills, speed, strength and weight.

WILL LEADING THE LEAGUE IN STATS HELP ME GET NOTICED?

Not necessarily, coaches know stats can be misleading so they don't base evaluations heavily off of them. Sure, if you lead the league, it might help you get "noticed" or your foot in the door. They may send you a questionnaire or ask the coaches in the area about you—but they'll evaluate your position-specific skills, size and speed over stats any day.

In all sports and in every position, from my experience, coaches aren't looking at numbers nearly as much as they are looking at your position-specific skills (burst, ball security, blocking, power, ability to break tackles, vision, lateral movement, cutting, acceleration, footwork), size and speed. They are also looking for the intangibles: toughness, leadership, ability to make plays. Are you a winner?

Coaches like to evaluate players against great competition, they want to see how you perform versus the best players in the area, state and region. Always remember that! Coaches may take a look at stats but their next question is: "What is the quality of competition they're up against?" Stats are relative! Always learn to play at the highest level that you can.

So yes, if you play in a successful, competitive conference and are the leading scorer—some schools will take notice, and do further research. Which, if you are offered, can also lead to other schools doing their research too. It's possible to get the ball rolling that way.

Ultimately, college coaches are looking for players who can help them win. What strengths can you bring to your unit, what can you do to help them win (not necessarily only with touches).

ONE SPORT VS. DUAL SPORT PLAYERS
The only thing that matters to the coaches recruiting you is how they evaluate you within their sport.

When recruiting dual-sport athletes to a college, coaches from multiple teams may help each other out and express interest from each sport. That doesn't normally mean you will get to play both sports at the collegiate level though, most coaches are greedy and will want you to focus year-round on their sport.

So yes, playing multiple sports can show coaches that you have general athletic ability but when it comes to offering scholarships, they only truly care about your athletic abilities in their sport. If you are talented enough in both to make the team legitimately, they'll take you!

TRUST IS EARNED THROUGH EVERY DAY HARD WORK, IT IS REALLY THAT SIMPLE.

CAN YOU QUALIFY ACADEMICALLY
The first question a college coach will ask once they are sold on you as a player is, "Can they get into school academically?"

Before you will be able to accept an athletic scholarship, practice and compete you will need to register with the NCAA Eligibility Center and have your academic and amateur status verified. We will be going into depth about the NCAA Eligibility Center and their standards shortly, but understand that it is critical to plan academically and take your schoolwork seriously.

Admission requirements do vary greatly from school to school, even for athletes. You will have to meet standards within the Division (I, II, III) but possibly have to meet an even higher standard at particular schools. Just because you meet the Division I standards that doesn't mean you will meet a particular school's' standards.

Many players may shoot to qualify academically for Division I but they may fall short of the Division II standards and not be eligible for those scholarships. It's best to aim higher academically

IF YOU ARE TRULY TRYING YOUR HARDEST, NEVER LOSE FAITH IN YOURSELF. JUST BECAUSE THE SHINE AND CROWDS AREN'T THERE (YET), THAT DOESN'T MEAN YOU AREN'T IMPROVING!

NCAA RECRUIT TIPS: 7 STEPS TO A SCHOLARSHIP

than to just meet the bottom standards, you may not get a Division I offer and then be stuck because you don't qualify academically for Division II.

Since recruiting is such a time-consuming process for coaches and they are constantly evaluating so many players, if they know you aren't even close to meeting the NCAA's and University's academic standards, they will likely drop you from their watch list and move on to the next player.

To most coaches, you aren't worth their time if they know it will be an issue to get you into school academically. Coaches simply don't have the time to battle for you, it's a process of appeals and special considerations that takes months of attention. Just so you know, in several cases, coaches are also recruiting other players with your same talent who are on track to have the grades to easily qualify.

Academic advisors at many universities may request transcripts of prospective student-athletes from coaches in order to project or predict how recruits will finish high school academically or what deficiencies they will need to take care of while planning for their senior year. They may even have standards in place that can end your recruitment or put your official visit on hold if they don't believe you will academically qualify.

Be sure to use the NCAA Eligibility Center code of 9999 when you register for the SAT or ACT to ensure that all of your scores are reported directly to the NCAA Eligibility Center from the testing agencies. Test scores that appear on transcripts will not be accepted!

It is also important to remember that the NCAA GPA (grade point average) is calculated using NCAA core courses only, be sure to look at your high school's 'List of NCAA Courses' on the NCAA Eligibility Center's website. These courses generally fall into the categories of math, science, English, social studies and foreign language. Only courses that appear on your school's list will be used in the calculation of the core GPA!

In my experiences, players aren't held back academically because of a lack of intelligence but rather a lack of effort. Don't let this be you! Your school, the ACT/SAT and college coaches can work with you if you have learning disabilities, concentration problems or credit deficiencies but you must address these issues as soon as possible!

NO STONE UNTURNED

One of the most common questions or worries that I hear is, "Help, I live in the middle of nowhere, nobody will ever find me" or "My team sucks, nobody will ever come to my school to scout me."

WRONG! This is one of the biggest misconceptions out there!

First off, one of my goals in sharing all of this behind-the-scenes information with you is to get you to stop making excuses and begin to 'find a way' in anything and everything that you do.

Secondly, coaches MUST have a reason to come scout your games or practice—they will rarely just show up unless you play for a powerhouse program that turns out Division I player after Division I player. Of the nine reasons why a coach may begin recruiting you— only one touches on a coach observing you at your high school… so RELAX! There are many other ways to get noticed!

Not all of the players that I've seen sign scholarships over the years were players that our staff found and went after. A good percentage of them were players who came to us first! Players who called us, sent us their highlight videos, showed up on campus, attended our camps. Many players who are getting recruited got the process going for themselves, they didn't wait for a coach to come find them!

Scholarship offers may not just come FIND you… for many of you, you will have to go FIND them!

Many of the coaches that I've worked with are looking for three base traits—skill, size and speed. Many players may only have two of these three traits or they may even only be masters of one. It's up to you to become the greatest that you can be at these three traits and recognize that sometimes you can't control all of these factors… but you can compensate by being really great at the others. After those three key traits, coaches are looking at your intangibles: toughness, leadership, intelligence, a relentless attitude and the ability to make things happen. There are a lot of slow, short players who go on to play at the collegiate level because they find a way to bring value to their high school team by being really great at one or two of these characteristics. You must focus on your skills, size and speed.

There are plenty of players that have these key qualities that coaches are looking for that are on losing teams in the middle of nowhere! There are great players who attend schools that haven't EVER produced a player before them who went on to play on the collegiate level. Even if you play in the middle of nowhere and your team can't win a game, that won't necessarily stop you from getting recruited if you have great skill, size, speed, toughness, leadership, intelligence, a relentless attitude and the ability to make things happen.

While many great players can go unrecruited or under recognized, it is also important to understand that coaches are constantly searching for that next great unknown. They're scouting the area, asking everyone about the next up-and-coming player.

Over and over I've heard coaches say, "I want tremendous players who are winners." This doesn't directly mean they want a player who comes from a school that has produced a lot of Division I players, it means that they are looking for players who come from a CULTURE OF WINNING, players who know how to prepare, players who picked up great habits from successful mentors, who are competitive, who don't make excuses and who won't settle.

Once you get that taste of WINNING... it's addictive. The more of the big games that you have won, the more you will begin to see the game in a different light. You begin to understand what it actually takes to win consistently. You understand the routine, the process. Coaches are looking for players who have already tasted success and want more.

IF YOU FOCUS MORE TIME ON YOUR FUNDAMENTALS AND LEADERSHIP THAN YOUR INTERNET RANKINGS... SUCCESS WILL COME!

Coaches want to know: "Do you understand what it takes to win and are you prepared to make those sacrifices?" What does this mean to you? It means that you can break the mold at your school by being the first player to be able to sign a college scholarship AND it means you can help be the player who helps create that 'winning attitude' at your school. It is up to you and your teammates (not just your coaches) to create a 'Culture of Winning.'

If you are an underclassman, start now and work to be the ONE who initiates the offseason workouts and who encourages their teammates to join them— BE A LEADER. Help create that culture of winning through your work ethic, toughness and by building chemistry within your team.

Prepare to have some thick skin and start going after what you want! Starting right now! Give coaches a reason to come find you.

FROM BUILDING WATCH LISTS TO FIRST DAY OF CLASS

Like life, like nature, recruiting follows a cycle. There is an information-gathering period, an evaluation period, a getting-to-know-you stage, an offer, a woo-ing stage and a closing stage. At each stage, coaches drop players from their list and begin to narrow down their top targets to a group that they will focus their time and energy on. Here is a quick overview of the cycle:

INFORMATION GATHERING - (FRESHMAN/SOPHOMORE):
- Building a Watch List for each graduating class with any potential athlete that would be a fit for the program, as early as freshman year (See 8 Reasons Why Players May Be Recruited)
- Sending questionnaires, updating contact and school info in the database

EVALUATION PERIOD (SOPHOMORE/JUNIOR/SENIOR):
- Calling prep coaches in assigned areas to find out more about the players on current Watch Lists, also adding new unknown players coaches may recommend
- Reviewing highlight videos and game film
- Traveling to games or tournaments to evaluate players in person
- Inviting players to camps or clinics
- Inviting players to games, Junior Days or unofficial visits
- Evaluating transcripts and grades
- Using social media accounts to learn more about players personalities and mindset on the recruiting process
- Discovering any red flags about prospective student-athletes concerning grades, character or attitudes
- Sending mail and academic information to prospects

GETTING-TO-KNOW STAGE (JUNIOR/SENIOR):
- Getting to know your selection factors, decision timeline and the people who will be helping you make your decision
- Calling you, your family, your mentors and your coaches to stay up-to-date with your life, often non-athletic conversations. The NCAA regulates when and how often college coaches may call you and your family, these rules vary by sport (see page 88).
- Showing up at your games to show support
- Building relationships with you and everyone that is important with you and who could help you make the decision
- Sending you more personalized academic info, athletic info and personal notes
- Inviting you to campus for an Official or Unofficial Visit- giving you a campus tour, invitation to a campus event or athletic event and making you feel at home
- Answering questions that you may have about their program, university, depth chart and situation. Recruiting is a two-way street and if they are sincerely interested in you, they want you to be just as excited about the decision as they are
- Encouraging you to register with the NCAA Eligibility Center

NCAA RECRUIT TIPS: 7 STEPS TO A SCHOLARSHIP

SCHOLARSHIP OFFER (SOPHOMORE/JUNIOR/SENIOR):
 - As a staff, the head coach will discuss your skills, size, speed, intangibles and academics with the assistant coaches and make a decision to offer you a scholarship. They rank, by position, their preference of players. They play the waiting game of waiting on their top choice to get their commitment, if they aren't getting an immediate yes they will keep their options open. Coaches are often conservative in deciding to offer a player a scholarship.

WOO-ING STAGE:
 - After extending a scholarship offer, coaches will begin putting the press on you, throwing stats and impressive facts at you and will do everything they can do to market their program to you. They want you to feel at home and feel like you are surrounded by family.

CLOSING THE DEAL:
 - Official Visits, paid for by the athletic department
 - In-Home Visits, where coaches make a trip to your house to seal the deal and get a commitment
 - Finalizing the official National Letter of Intent paperwork
 - Finalizing test scores and transcripts in order for you to qualify academically
 - Finalizing all information with the NCAA Clearinghouse
 - Finalizing university admissions, housing and scheduling paperwork

FIRST DAY OF CLASS!

"TELL ME MORE ABOUT YOURSELF..." - ANSWERING INTERVIEW-STYLE QUESTIONS OF COACHES

The recruiting process makes a lot of prospects and their families very anxious — the stakes are enormous, the competition is tough and emotions are running high. And for most coaches who have been in the business for a couple years, this is something they do every day, all day – it's something they can do in their sleep.

But understand, when coaches are asking you questions (especially personal, non-athletic questions) they are simply trying to get to know more about you. They're trying to make you feel comfortable, working to build a relationship with you and your circle of family and friends. They want to know what you like/dislike so if they want to move forward with the recruiting process, they know how to sell their program to you. They'll ask you what your favorite food is, who your favorite pro player is, favorite sneaker brand, favorite vacation spot, favorite music artist– they're just trying to get to know you and use that information to build a relationship and to find ways to sell their program, university, city and personality to you.

Relax and just be honest with them, tell them more about yourself (believe me, they've heard it all) and what you're looking for. There are no wrong answers. You don't have to fit a stereotype of a certain type of athlete to be taken serious– there is a wide range of interests and personalities of players, so coaches are just trying to figure out what type of person you are. They can watch your film and talk to your coaches to determine how you would fit in as an athlete; next they're trying to figure out what your vibe is as a person and how you would fit in with their lockerroom. But again, there are no wrong answers; all teams have a wide range of personalities.

Two ways to ace this part of the process, besides from just being honest: Don't let mom or dad answer every question for you, and ask the coaches questions too! Coaches want to hear directly from you and get to know you personally without mom interjecting everything she thinks they'd want to hear. Coaches also like players who can carry a conversation with them, and ask them questions as well — it's often a sign of maturity when players can feel comfortable, hold a conversation and ask questions too.

HOW TO CARRY YOURSELF WHEN APPROACHING COACHES

As you prepare to contact schools, realize that you need to present yourself in a polished way when speaking to college coaches. College coaches are professionals; they may wear sneakers and t-shirts at practice but most of them wear ties or polos at work, and slacks and dress shoes in the office. I get weekly phone calls from players saying, "Aye, aye.... Write this name down. Yo, John Smith. Write that name down."

Just so you know, I don't even pick up a pen. If you're THAT good, we already have your name in the system and are trying to get in contact with YOU. Or my favorite, "Who's the head coach? Yeah, yeah... Coach Jefferson, let me talk to Steve..."

That extra attitude, ego and unprofessionalism will get you nowhere!
First off, you called us and you shouldn't EVER refer to a coach by their first name. Ever. If you're really interested in a school, look up the head coach's name before you call. Your first goal is to have the person that answers the phone take you serious, and that starts with being polite and organized. When you contact schools, make sure that you:
- Speak up, speak clearly and don't mumble
- Know the head coach's name before you call or even better, have a list of all of the coaches in front of you so you can make sure you get the name right. Never ask for them by their first name.
- Ask which assistant coach recruits your area and get their name, direct office number and email address. Double-check the spelling and keep notes!
- Spell your name out if leaving a message and repeat your phone number twice. If we can't understand the phone number, nobody can call back!
- If necessary, set up a different email address for recruiting purposes. I can't tell you how many inappropriate email addresses (and Twitter names) I've come across over the years, and ladies, you are just as bad! Keep it simple with your name and jersey number. Also, no mascot names in your email address. If you are Gamecock17@recruit.com, do you

think the Clemson and North Carolina coaches will take you serious? Keep it simple: jen15@hotmail.com, bobbysmith@gmail.com or shortstopsam@yahoo.com.

- Depending on your grade, understand that a coach may not be able to respond to you. Rules vary for each sport as far as when coaches are able to contact you so check NCAA.org for that information.
- When you are using form letters, triple check that you have changed everything. I can't tell you how many letters I have received from prospects who in the first line confessed that they were "dreaming of" playing for our biggest rival. We all know coaches AND recruits send form letters, just make sure to check that each separate packet is correct before you mail them!
- If you are meeting a coach, dress appropriately. Nothing will make a coach take notice quicker than if you are wearing a tie and collared shirt or polo. Same for the ladies—cover up and dress for church instead of dressing for the club! Sure, it's okay if you wear something more casual, but coaches will take ANY player serious if they present themselves in a professional way.

QUESTIONS ABOUT PLAYING TIME

Playing time is a common decision factor for a lot of players, coaches are well aware most players want to come into the program with a starting job or play consistent minutes right away.

A better question to ask is, "How many players, at my position, in my signing class, do you plan to sign?"

For starters, no matter what a coach tells you during the recruiting process, there is no such thing as a guaranteed starting job. Never make a decision solely based on this factor because coaches have been known to stretch the truth about playing time. You are usually getting the sugar-coated answer to this question until you sign that NLI (National Letter of Intent) and enroll in school. And honestly, they won't entirely be sure until they've had you go through pre-season workouts and see how you are adjusting being away from home.

Coaches love competitors so they know that MOST of their signees are going to be thinking they are deserving of significant and early playing time. But, coaches also get funny if a player comes off as selfish—which is how some coaches may read that question.

Better ways to address the playing time topic:
- "How many players, at my position, in my signing class, do you plan to sign?"
- "What role do you see me playing next year?"
- "What is the plan for my development from HS to freshman year? Freshman year to sophomore year? Upperclassmen years?"

- What does the depth chart look like for my freshman season?

With coaches, you need to take the approach that you are willing to put in the work and do anything to help the TEAM win, not necessarily focus on your minutes or stats.

KEEPING YOUR RECRUITING COACHES UPDATED ON WHO HAS OFFERED YOU

Is it ok to tell the coaches who are recruiting you if another school offers you too? Yes, in fact many coaches will ask you what schools you have offers from in your early conversations. As the process moves on, coaches most likely will continue to ask you which schools have offered, which schools have come to see you play or invited you to games/camps.

Coaches want to know who their competition is. But more importantly, as you tell them which schools have offered you or are showing interest, they are trying to learn more about your likes and dislikes. As you discuss these offers and visits coaches are learning more about what eliminates programs from consideration and what factors move schools up on your list.

- Do you want to stay close to home, or go far away? Will distance play any factor?
- Do you want to play in a certain conference?
- Do you want to go to a big school?
- Do you want to live in a major city or would you prefer to live in a college town environment?
- Is playing time a major factor?

You aren't bragging, you are being open and honest, a trait you should expect from the coaches recruiting you. You don't have to send out a mass text or email anytime you get an offer or visit from a coach but it is ok (and encouraged) to tell your recruiting coaches in conversations or be honest if they ask.

TRUTH:
SCHOLARSHIP OFFERS
ARE NOT GIVEN...
THEY ARE EARNED!

NCAA RECRUIT TIPS: 7 STEPS TO A SCHOLARSHIP

WHAT TO EXPECT: FRESHMAN YEAR OF HS

:: FOCUS ON FUNDAMENTALS... within your sport and become a master of those! Don't worry about the recruiting process; focus all of your energy on being the best player that you can be and on being a great leader and teammate. The better you play, the better your odds are of being discovered! Put 100% effort into your fundamentals—even if you are on the JV or Freshman team!

:: PLAY HARD... Nearly every school in nearly every sport relies on regional or national scouting services. Universities pay an annual fee for reports from established scouts, especially for information on top freshmen and sophomores. Each service normally provides contact info and a short 10-word-or-less description of the athletes' style of play, and ranks them with a letter or category grade (Division I, II, III, NAIA). These reports are scanned for sizes, speeds, stats and notes from observations. Be aware that there are eyes everywhere—not just the college coaches themselves!
(LOW/MID/HIGH LEVEL PLAYERS)

:: FOCUS ON YOUR GRADES... and set good study habits. Set aside time for homework each day. Your freshman and sophomore grades will be heavily evaluated when you are a junior. Get off to a great start.

:: MAKE SURE YOUR GRADES EXCEED THE 'NCAA SLIDING SCALE' STANDARDS
– Division I signees need to qualify academically based on their Core GPA and ACT/SAT test scores. Division II requires even higher SAT/ACT minimums. Even if you dream is to go Division I, have the grades to qualify for Division II as well, you don't want to miss out on additional scholarship opportunities. Additionally, each university sets their own academic standards which may be even higher than the NCAA Division I or Division II standards.

FRESHMAN YEAR, GET AHEAD BY...

:: ATTENDING SUMMER CAMPS OR CLINICS... at the schools that you are interested in and combines managed by third-parties (AAU, Nike, etc). Any regional or national tournaments or exposure events you can attend will be helpful. By attending as a younger player you can get over the anxiousness and uncertainty of the drills and be more polished as an upperclassman.

:: IF SENT A QUESTIONNAIRE BY A SCHOOL... fill it out and return it promptly! It is a sign of interest, RESPOND!

WHAT TO EXPECT: SOPHOMORE YEAR OF HS

:: **FOCUS ON FUNDAMENTALS...** within your sport and become a master of those! Don't worry about the recruiting process; focus all of your energy on being the best player that you can be and on being a great leader and teammate. The better you play and the more games your team wins, the better your odds are of being discovered! Put 100% effort into your fundamentals—even if you are on the JV team!

:: **FOCUS ON YOUR GRADES...** and set good study habits. Set aside time for homework each day. Your sophomore grades will be heavily evaluated when you are a junior. You don't want grades to be a factor that eliminates you off of a coach's 'watch list' later down the road.

:: **MAKE SURE YOUR GRADES EXCEED THE 'NCAA SLIDING SCALE' STANDARDS** – Division I signees need to qualify academically based on their Core GPA and ACT/SAT test scores. Division II requires even higher SAT/ACT minimums. Even if you dream is to go Division I, have the grades to qualify for Division II as well, you don't want to miss out on all of those additional scholarship opportunities. Additionally, each university sets their own student-athlete academic standards which may be even higher than the NCAA Division I or Division II standards.

:: **IF SENT A QUESTIONNAIRE BY A SCHOOL...** fill it out and return it promptly! It is a sign of interest, RESPOND!

:: **AFTER YOUR SOPHOMORE SEASON IT IS A GOOD IDEA TO BEGIN TO TAKE THE ACT OR SAT TEST...** By testing early, it will give you an idea of what subjects you need to make improvements in during the next few years. Check with your coach or guidance counselor, there are NCAA standards (and different standards at each university) that must be met with your GPA and your ACT/SAT test scores. If you are financially unable to afford the ACT/SAT tests, check with your coach or guidance counselor for a financial waiver! Most schools REQUIRE a copy of your ACT/SAT/PSAT scores before allowing you to make an official visit.

:: **PLAY HARD...** As a sophomore, you are too young to contact but coaches may begin doing their homework on you if you are a top player in the area. It is still very early in the process, but some college staffs work ahead by beginning their research on recruiting classes a couple years in advance. Coaches may call around to find out more about your talent level, how you compete vs. local players and if there are red flags concerning your character or academic standing as early as your sophomore year.

Nearly every school in nearly every sport relies on regional or national scouting services. Universities pay an annual fee for reports from established scouts, especially for information on top freshmen and sophomores. Each service normally provides contact info and a short 10-word-or-less description of the athletes' style of play, and ranks them with a letter or category grade (Division I, II, III, NAIA). These reports are scanned for sizes, speeds, stats and notes from observations. Be aware that there are eyes everywhere—not just the college coaches themselves!
(LOW/MID/HIGH LEVEL PLAYERS)

NCAA RECRUIT TIPS: 7 STEPS TO A SCHOLARSHIP

Coaches will begin noting top underclassmen to add to the database for future recruitment as they attend practices or tournaments. Be aware that they are watching and making notes, even if they aren't able to contact you. (HIGH/MID/LOW LEVEL players)

Coaches will begin screening highlight video, stats, regional all-star teams and rankings for top regional players and may add underclassmen names to their watch lists for future recruitment. (HIGH INTEREST)

:: INVITE YOU TO CAMPUS... If you are an elite player in the area, coaches may be inviting your team to their summer camps or sports clinics as a sophomore. If financially possible, attend those at the universities you are interested in! Camps can be a very important step in the process for both the prospect and the coaching staff. (HIGH LEVEL)

As a prospect, they are able to offer you complimentary admission (via a pass list at the gate) for you and up to two guests. (MEDIUM/HIGH INTEREST)

SOPHOMORE YEAR, GET AHEAD BY...
:: ATTEND SUMMER CAMPS OR CLINICS... at the schools that you are interested in and combines managed by third-parties (AAU, Nike, etc). Any regional or national tournaments or exposure events you can attend will be helpful. By attending as a younger player you can get over the anxiousness and uncertainty of the drills and be more polished as an upperclassman.

:: BEING ACADEMICALLY ON TRACK... Sit down with your guidance counselor to make sure your course load is in line with NCAA (Division I and II standards) and university requirements. If you are aiming to attend an academically prestigious university, see what their typical freshman academic profile is. Yes, some schools are able to make exceptions in admissions for student-athletes, but many have a limited number of spots for the entire athletic department to use. Many universities do not have much wiggle room academically between the general student population and student-athletes. Be prepared!

WHAT TO EXPECT: JUNIOR YEAR OF HS

:: **FOCUS ON FUNDAMENTALS...** within your sport and become a master of those! Don't waste time worrying about the recruiting process, focus all of your energy on being the best player that you can be. If you are a top player, make sure you work on becoming a great leader and teammate—these are qualities coaches are looking for in addition to size and skill! The better you play and the more games your team wins, the better your odds are of being discovered! Put 100% effort into your fundamentals!

:: **IF SENT A QUESTIONNAIRE BY THE SCHOOL...** fill it out and return it promptly! It is a sign of interest, RESPOND!

:: **BE ON TRACK ACADEMICALLY...** Sit down with your guidance counselor to make sure your course load is in line with NCAA (Division I and Division II) and university requirements. If you are aiming to attend an academically prestigious university, see what their typical freshman academic profile is. Yes, some schools are able to make exceptions in admissions for student-athletes, but many have a limited number of spots for the entire athletic department to use. Many universities do not have much wiggle room academically between the general student population and student-athletes. Be prepared!

:: **MAKE ARRANGEMENTS TO TAKE THE ACT OR SAT TEST** – it is MANDATORY! Check with your coach or guidance counselor, there are NCAA standards (and different standards at each university) that must be met with your GPA and your ACT/SAT test scores. If you are financially unable to afford the ACT/SAT tests, check with your coach or guidance counselor for a financial waiver! Most schools REQUIRE a copy of your ACT/SAT/PSAT scores before allowing you to make an official visit.

:: **MAKE SURE YOUR GRADES EXCEED THE 'NCAA SLIDING SCALE' STANDARDS**

– Division I signees need to qualify academically based on their Core GPA and ACT/SAT test scores. Division II requires even higher SAT/ACT minimums. Even if you dream is to go Division I, have the grades to qualify for Division II as well, you don't want to miss out on all of those additional scholarship opportunities.
Additionally, each university sets their own student-athlete academic standards which may be even higher than the NCAA Division I or Division II standards.

:: **REGISTER FOR THE NCAA CLEARINGHOUSE** - All prospective student-athletes MUST register with the NCAA Eligibility Center (www.EligibilityCenter.org) in order to practice, play and receive a Division I or Division II athletic scholarship. The NCAA Eligibility Center oversees the certification process to confirm academic credentials and amateurism status. The NCAA Eligibility Center determines if players are ruled eligible, and able to compete and accept a scholarship. High school students can register with the NCAA Eligibility Center at any time but it is recommended that you begin the process during your junior year. Prospective student-athletes must submit transcripts from all schools attended, report SAT/ACT scores directly from the testing agency (use code 9999 when registering for the tests to have your scores sent) and submit the $80 fee. The Eligibility Center confirms that #1- you have graduated, #2- have completed the required number of core courses (varies depending on Division I or II and graduation year), #3- earned a minimum GPA, #4- earned a qualifying SAT/ACT score and #5- completed an amateurism questionnaire and #6- have requested final amateurism certification.

NCAA RECRUIT TIPS: 7 STEPS TO A SCHOLARSHIP

:: **ATTEND SUMMER CAMPS OR CLINICS...** at schools that you are interested in and combines managed by third-parties (AAU, Nike, etc). Any regional or national tournaments or exposure events you can attend will be helpful.

:: **YOU MAY BEGIN RECEIVING MAIL...** cards, letters, emails and information on the university and program. If you begin to receive this information from schools it means you are on their watch list and they need more information on you and to see you play, either in person or on video before they can determine if you are a candidate for a scholarship. The date when schools may begin contacting you varies by sport, check NCAA.org for more info. (Low-High Interest From Coaches)

:: **IN-PERSON VISITS...** If you are a priority recruit, coaches will come to your school as NCAA periods allow – they will watch practice, meet with your coach and show their face around school to let you know they're interested. As a junior, a college coach may not make in-person contact (speak) with you off their campus but may make academic or athletic evaluations. (MEDIUM/HIGH Interest From   Coach)

:: **REQUEST TRANSCRIPT...** If interested, coaches may request a copy of your transcript from your coach or guidance counselor to determine if you would be able to pass their academic standards (university and athletic department standards). Coaches are actively recruiting several players and don't want to waste a lot of time if they know you would not be able to get admitted into their university or fit their basic standards. Many athletic departments have academic advisors who evaluate your current grades and make projections on how you will finish high school. They may recommend terminating your recruitment if they don't believe you can qualify or believe that you can be successful there. (MEDIUM/HIGH Interest From Coach)

:: **ASKING AROUND ABOUT YOU...** Coaches may call around to find out more about what your decision factors are, talent level, how you compete vs. local players and if there are red flags concerning your character or academic standing. They will call everyone to get a better picture of you as a player, student and person— your HS coaches, AAU coach, parents, prep coaches in your region or conference, guidance counselor, mentors, brothers, sisters or even other college coaches. (HIGH INTEREST)

:: **MONITORING YOUR SOCIAL MEDIA...** Coaches will likely be checking out your social media pages to find out more about you, what other schools you are visiting or being offered by and your thoughts on the process. Many coaches also use social media as the quickest way to communicate with you. Be aware they take into consideration your language, attitude and how you carry yourself. Nearly every coach I know has eliminated players from their watch list because of negativity from their Facebook or Twitter accounts. (HIGH INTEREST)

:: **EVALUATIONS & CONTACTS** – Each coach is allowed a set number of evaluations and contacts with each prospect per year, beginning the prospect's junior year. If they are doing their homework on you or are interested, they will attend your games and practices and set up times to visit with your high school coach or guidance counselor. [Basic Definition - Evaluation: Any off-campus activity designed to assess the academic qualifications or athletics ability (during which no contact occurs) of a prospective student-athlete / Contact: Any face-to-face encounter between a prospective student-athlete or the prospective student- athlete's parents, relatives or legal guardians and an institutional staff member or athletics representative during which any dialogue occurs in excess of an exchange of a greeting.]- (HIGH INTEREST)

:: **GET YOU TO CAMPUS...** If coaches have developed some interest (not necessarily have made a decision to offer you a scholarship yet), they will try to get you to campus for an unofficial visit (expenses paid by prospect). Some unofficial visits are set up with individual players and are more personalized or others are Junior Days where hundreds of athletes are invited. They want to get to know you better, show you what they have to offer in terms of campus and facilities, give you an opportunity to get to know their players and introduce you to academic programs that you may be interested in. Recruiting is a two-way street so they are getting a read on your interest level and giving you an opportunity to get to know them better to see if they fit your needs. (MEDIUM/HIGH INTEREST)

Coaches may invite you to campus for games. As a prospect, they are able to offer you complimentary admission (via a pass list at the gate) for you and up to two guests. (MEDIUM/HIGH INTEREST)

:: **UNDERSTANDING YOUR INTEREST LEVEL...** Coaches will be asking you where else you have made unofficial visits to in order to gauge your interest level with their school. They may ask you what you liked or didn't like about the other schools you are looking at. If you are a rated player, most coaches learn about your unofficial visits on the internet so be prepared that they will ask you about your thoughts on the competition, you haven't done anything wrong—they just want to figure out your likes and dislikes and selection criteria. (HIGH INTEREST)

:: **INFORMATION ON MAJORS YOU ARE INTERESTED IN...** If coaches have a high interest in you, they may send you specific information on the academic major that interests you. They want to make sure you and your family know they are interested in you outside of just sports. (HIGH INTEREST)

:: **PLAY HARD...** Coaches will be evaluating highlight videos, stats, regional all-star teams and rankings of juniors. This is a key year for you as a player! Following your junior season, send your highlight video and Student-Athlete Resume (stats, measurements, accomplishments, awards, grades and contact information) to schools you are interested in via mail or email. (MEDIUM/HIGH INTEREST)

Nearly every school in nearly every sport relies on regional or national scouting services. Universities pay an annual fee for reports from established scouts. Each service normally provides contact info and a short 10-word-or-less description of the athletes' style of play, and ranks them with a letter or category grade (Division I, II, III, NAIA). These reports are scanned for sizes, speeds, stats and notes from observations and upperclassmen we may not have been aware of. Be aware that there are eyes everywhere—not just the college coaches themselves!
(LOW/MID/HIGH LEVEL PLAYERS)

:: **SUMMER CAMPS...** If you are a recommended player or on their 'watch list,' coaches may be personally inviting you to their summer camps or sports clinics. If financially possible, attend those at the universities you are interested in! Camps can be a very important step in the process for both the prospect and the coaching staff.
(LOW/MEDIUM/HIGH INTEREST)

NCAA RECRUIT TIPS: 7 STEPS TO A SCHOLARSHIP

:: **PHONE CALLS...** Depending on your sport, coaches may begin contacting you at some point during or after your junior year. If coaches have a high interest in you, they will likely be calling you the maximum number of times per week or month as allowed by the NCAA for your sport. The NCAA limits them in the number of times they are able to initiate phone calls with you, but you are able to call them as often as you would like. The dates when coaches may begin calling you and the frequency of calls varies by sport and is determined by the NCAA. Check NCAA.org for more info. (MEDIUM/HIGH INTEREST)

:: **IN-PERSON CONTACTS...** If you have been offered by a school and are a top priority for them, they will go out of their way to express their interest in you by showing up at your games and practices. There are times when coaches are making face-to-face contacts and in-person evaluations at your games to merely show support, understand that their time is very valuable and they are making a commitment to you by being present. (HIGH INTEREST)

:: **BUILDING RELATIONSHIPS...** Coaches understand that you are likely influenced (sometimes heavily) by your family, friends, coaches and mentors. Along with building a relationship with you, they are often building just as important relationships with those in your circle. If they are making this effort, understand you are a high priority to them. (HIGH INTEREST)

:: **COACHES MAY BE TRYING TO UNDERSTAND THE DYNAMICS WITHIN YOUR FAMILY** – if you are close-knit, have a need to stay close-to-home or if you are comfortable going away to school in another state. They are evaluating your family situation and the possibility of you realistically choosing their school. (HIGH INTEREST)

:: **IF YOU HAVE ACADEMIC, ATTITUDE OR CHARACTER RED-FLAGS...** coaches are constantly evaluating the risk-reward during recruitment. Are you worth the trouble based on your past actions, and are you making improvements in those areas and maturing? Are you worth the risk to them or are there other players just as talented who have zero red flags? (MEDIUM/HIGH INTEREST)

JUNIOR YEAR – GET AHEAD BY...

:: **START CONTACTING SCHOOLS ON YOUR OWN...** If you haven't gotten much interest by the end of your junior year, you should start contacting schools on your own. Don't panic- you still have PLENTY of time! It is best to start with local or state schools (even if those aren't your first choice) and build interest instead of starting at the FBS Top 25 programs. Send your highlights, stats, awards, accomplishments and contact information to schools within an hour or two and follow-up within a week with someone personally on the phone. Find out which coach on staff recruits your geographic region or position—your overall goal is to get your highlight video in their hands and to get them to watch it and give you feedback. Since most schools first question to you will be "Who have you been offered by?" – it is easier to begin generating interest or offers from local or smaller schools than by contacting national Top 25 teams.

:: **SET UP UNOFFICIAL VISITS AFTER YOUR SEASON...** If you fit the athletic standards of a school, your junior year is a good time to take as many unofficial visits as possible to the schools that you are seriously interested in. Financially, it may not be an option but if it is, the only way to really decide if you like a school or program is to visit it in person. In several regions, you are able to visit many universities and colleges within a manageable drive. The quantity of schools that you visit isn't important, but rather the quality of programs that fit your needs and skill level. You may not like them in person or your interest may double or triple after making a visit. Definitely get in touch with the recruiting coach before your visit and tell them you would like to check out the campus and try to set up a meeting in advance if possible.

WHAT TO EXPECT: SENIOR YEAR OF HS

:: FOCUS ON FUNDAMENTALS... within your sport and become a master of those! Focus your energy on being the best player that you can be. Coaches at every program are looking for great players. It's never too late, even after Signing Day, there are still opportunities. If you are a top player, make sure you work on becoming a great leader and teammate—these are qualities that coaches are looking for in addition to size and skill! The better you play and the more games your team wins, the better your odds are of being discovered! Put 100% effort into your fundamentals!

:: IF SENT A QUESTIONNAIRE BY A SCHOOL... fill it out and return it promptly! It is a sign of interest, RESPOND!

:: MAKE ARRANGEMENTS TO TAKE THE ACT OR SAT TEST – it is MANDATORY! Check with your coach or guidance counselor, there are NCAA standards (and different standards at each university) that must be met with your GPA and your ACT/SAT test scores. If you are financially unable to afford the ACT/SAT tests, check with your coach or guidance counselor for a financial waiver! Most schools REQUIRE a copy of your ACT/SAT/PSAT scores before allowing you to make an official visit.

:: MAKE SURE YOUR GRADES EXCEED THE 'NCAA SLIDING SCALE' STANDARDS – Division I signees need to qualify academically based on their Core GPA and ACT/SAT test scores. Division II requires even higher SAT/ACT minimums. Even if you dream is to go Division I, have the grades to qualify for Division II as well, you don't want to miss out on all of those additional scholarship opportunities.

Additionally, each university sets their own student-athlete academic standards which may be even higher than the NCAA Division I or Division II standards.

:: ATTEND SUMMER CAMPS OR CLINICS... at the schools you are interested in and combines managed by third-parties (AAU, Nike, etc). Any regional or national tournaments or exposure events you can attend will be helpful.

:: REGISTER FOR THE NCAA CLEARINGHOUSE - All prospective student-athletes MUST register with the NCAA Eligibility Center (www.EligibilityCenter.org) in order to practice, play and receive a Division I or Division II athletic scholarship. The NCAA Eligibility Center oversees the certification process to confirm academic credentials and amateurism status. The NCAA Eligibility Center determines if players are ruled eligible, and able to compete and accept a scholarship. High school students can register with the NCAA Eligibility Center at any time but it is recommended that you begin the process during your junior year. Prospective student-athletes must submit transcripts from all schools attended, report SAT/ACT scores directly from the testing agency (use code 9999 when registering for the tests to have your scores sent) and submit the $80 fee. The Eligibility Center confirms that #1- you have graduated, #2- have completed the required number of core courses (varies depending on

NCAA RECRUIT TIPS: 7 STEPS TO A SCHOLARSHIP

Division I or II and graduation year), #3- earned a minimum GPA, #4- earned a qualifying SAT/ACT score and #5- completed an amateurism questionnaire and #6- have requested final amateurism certification.

:: **YOU MAY BEGIN RECEIVING MAIL...** cards, letters, emails and information on the university and program. If you begin to receive this information from schools it means you are on their watch list and they need more information on you and to see you play, either in person or on video before they can determine if you are a candidate for a scholarship. (Low-High Interest From Coaches)

If you fit the athletic standards of a school, the summer before your senior year is a good time to take as many unofficial visits as possible to the schools that you are seriously interested in. (Note: In men's and women's basketball, there are restrictions for unofficial visits during July, check with the NCAA or each university before planning a trip.) Financially, it may not be an option but if it is, the only way to really decide if you like a school or program is to visit it in person. In several regions, you are able to visit many universities and colleges within a manageable drive. The quantity of schools that you visit isn't important, but rather the quality of programs that fit your needs. You may not like them in person or your interest may double or triple after making a visit. If you haven't been in contact with a member of the coaching staff yet but are interested, contact the school first and ask for the coach who recruits your geographic area. Get in touch with the recruiting coach before your visit and tell them you would like to check out the campus and try to set up a meeting in advance if possible.

:: **IN-PERSON VISITS...** If you are a priority recruit, coaches will come to your school as NCAA periods allow – they will watch practice, meet with your coach, show their face around school to let you know they're interested. Depending on the team of year they may not be able to contact (speak to you in-person) but can evaluate your academic and athletic abilities. (MEDIUM/HIGH Interest From Coach)

:: **REQUEST TRANSCRIPT...** If interested, coaches may request a copy of your transcript from your coach or guidance counselor to determine if you would be able to pass their academic standards (university and athletic department standards). Coaches are actively recruiting several players and don't want to waste a lot of time if they know you would not be able to get admitted into their university or fit their basic standards. Many athletic departments have academic advisors who evaluate your current grades and make projections on how you will finish high school. They may recommend terminating your recruitment if they don't believe you can be successful there. (MEDIUM/HIGH Interest From Coach)

:: **ASKING AROUND ABOUT YOU...** Coaches will call around to find out more about what your decision factors are, talent level, how you compete vs. local players and if there are red flags concerning your character or academic standing. They will call everyone to get a better picture of you as a player, student and person—your HS coaches, AAU coach, parents, prep coaches in your region or conference, guidance counselor, mentors, brothers, sisters or even other college coaches. (HIGH INTEREST)

:: **MONITORING YOUR SOCIAL MEDIA...** Coaches will likely be checking out your social media pages to find out more about you, what other schools you are visiting or being offered by and your thoughts on the process. Many coaches also use social media as the quickest way to communicate with you. Be aware they take into consideration your language, attitude and how you carry yourself. Nearly every coach I know has eliminated players from their list because of negativity from their Facebook or Twitter accounts. (HIGH INTEREST)

:: **EVALUATIONS & CONTACTS** – Each coach is allowed a set number of evaluations and contacts with each prospect per year, beginning the prospect's junior year. If they are doing their homework on you or interested, they will attend your games and practices and set up times to visit with your high school coach or guidance counselor. [Basic Definition - Evaluation: Any off-campus activity designed to assess the academic qualifications or athletics ability (during which no contact occurs) of a prospective student-athlete / Contact: Any face-to-face encounter between a prospective student-athlete or the prospective student-athlete's parents, relatives or legal guardians and an institutional staff member or athletics representative during which any dialogue occurs in excess of an exchange of a greeting.] (HIGH INTEREST)

:: **SET UP IN-HOME VISIT...** If a coach has offered you and is hoping you will commit to their school, they will set up an in-home visit with your family. Each school is allowed only one in-home visit per prospective student-athlete. (HIGH INTEREST)

:: **SET UP OFFICIAL VISIT...** If coaches have offered you a scholarship, they will try to get you (and likely your family) to set up a date to make an official visit (expenses for prospect paid by school) to campus. Prospects are only able to visit up to five schools on official visits, and they may last up to a maximum of 48 hours. Some prospects come alone and others are joined by their extended family. (HIGH INTEREST)

:: **INFORMATION ON MAJORS YOU ARE INTERESTED IN...** If coaches have a high interest in you, they may send you specific information on the academic major that interests you. They want to make sure you and your family knows that they are interested in you beyond just sports. (HIGH INTEREST)

:: **INVITE YOU TO CAMPUS...** If there is a medium to high level of interest, coaches will invite you to campus for games. As a prospect, they are able to offer you complimentary admission (via a pass list at the gate) for you and up to two guests. (MEDIUM/HIGH INTEREST)

If you are a recommended player or on their 'watch list,' coaches may be personally inviting you to their summer camps or sports clinics. If financially possible, attend those at the universities you are interested in! Camps can be a very important step in the process for both the prospect and the coaching staff. (MEDIUM/HIGH INTEREST)

If coaches have developed some interest (not necessarily have made a decision to offer you a scholarship), they will try to get you to campus for an unofficial visit (expenses paid by prospect).

Some unofficial visits are schedule with individual players and are more personalized or others are open to hundreds of athletes and are much more informal. They want to get to know you better, show you what they have to offer in terms of campus and facilities, give you an opportunity to get to know their players and introduce you to academic programs you may be interested in.

PS_BX07271919

CreateSpace
222 Old Wire Rd
Columbia, SC 29172

Question About Your Order?
Log in to your account at www.createspace.com and "Contact Support."

09/16/2017 01:52:30 PM
Order ID: 186026150

Qty.	Item
	IN THIS SHIPMENT
1	NCAA Recruit Tips: 100 Most-Asked Recruiti... 150329188X
1	NCAA Recruit Tips: 7 Steps to a Scholarship 0985904879

NCAA RECRUIT TIPS: 7 STEPS TO A SCHOLARSHIP

Recruiting is a two-way street so they are getting a read on your interest level and giving you an opportunity to get to know them better to see if they fit your needs. (MEDIUM/HIGH INTEREST)

:: **PLAY HARD...** Coaches will still be evaluating highlight videos, stats, regional all-star teams and rankings of seniors. There is still time to pick up interests and offers from plenty of universities. During or immediately following your senior season, send your highlight video and/or stats, measurements, accomplishments, awards, grades and contact information to schools you are interested in via mail or email. Follow-up with each university that you are interested in and try to get a coach or recruiting coordinator on the phone to determine if they are interested or not.

Nearly every school in nearly every sport relies on regional or national scouting services. Universities pay an annual fee for reports from established scouts, especially for information on top freshmen and sophomores. Each service normally provides contact info and a short 10-word-or-less description of the athletes' style of play, and ranks them with a letter or category grade (Division I, II, III, NAIA). These reports are scanned for sizes, speeds, stats and notes from observations. Be aware that there are eyes everywhere—not just the college coaches themselves! (LOW/MID/HIGH LEVEL PLAYERS)

:: **PHONE CALLS...** If coaches have a high interest in you, they will likely be calling you the maximum number of times per week or month as allowed by the NCAA for your sport. The NCAA limits them in the number of times they are able to initiate phone calls with you, but you are able to call them as often as you would like. The dates when coaches may begin calling you and the frequency of calls varies by sport and is determined by the NCAA. (MEDIUM/HIGH INTEREST)

:: **IN-PERSON CONTACTS...** If you have been offered by a school and are a top priority for them, they will go out of their way to express their interest in you by showing up at your games and practices. There are times when coaches are making face-to-face contacts and in-person evaluations at your games to merely show support, understand that their time is very valuable and they are making a commitment to you by being present. (HIGH INTEREST)

:: **BUILDING RELATIONSHIPS...** Coaches understand that you are likely influenced (sometimes heavily) by your family, friends, coaches and mentors. Along with building a relationship with you, they are often building just as important relationships with those in your circle. If they are making this effort, understand you are a priority to them. (HIGH INTEREST)

If you are a priority recruit, coaches are getting to understand the dynamics within your family – if you are close-knit, have a need to stay close-to-home or if you are comfortable going away to school in another state. They are evaluating your family situation and the possibility of you realistically choosing their school. (HIGH INTEREST)

:: **IF YOU HAVE ACADEMIC, ATTITUDE OR CHARACTER RED-FLAGS...** Coaches are always evaluating the risk-reward of your recruitment. Are you worth the trouble based on your past actions, and are you making improvements in those areas and maturing? Are you worth the risk to them or are there other players just as talented who have zero red flags? (MEDIUM/HIGH INTEREST)

AS A SENIOR, YOU STILL CAN...
:: START CONTACTING SCHOOLS ON YOUR OWN... If you haven't gotten much interest by the beginning or end of your senior season, you should start contacting schools on your own. Don't panic- you still have time. It is best to start with local or state schools (even if those aren't your first choice) and build interest instead of starting at the BSC Top 25 programs. Send your highlight videos, stats, awards, accomplishments and contact information to schools within an hour or two and follow-up within a few weeks with someone personally on the phone. Find out which coach on staff recruits your geographic region or position—your overall goal is to get your highlight video in their hands and to get them to watch it and give you feedback. Since most schools first question to you will be "Who have you been offered by?" – it is easier to begin generating interest or offers from local schools than by contacting the defending national champions or elite national teams.

WHEN COLLEGE COACHES CAN CONTACT:
BY SPORT
Overall, NCAA rules restrict when coaches can call you, visit you in person, send you mail/email, etc. The rules do NOT restrict when prospects or their parents can contact coaches, outside of visiting in person during a Dead Period. You and your family can contact (email, call) coaches at any time. It's important to note, although you can call or write them, if you're too young for them to contact, which also means they can't respond, even if you initiate the contact. (For example, if you call and leave a voicemail for a coach, even if they are interested, they can't return your phone call.)

MEN'S BASKETBALL
SOPHOMORE YEAR - DIVISION I
RECRUITING MATERIALS:
- You may receive brochures for camps, questionnaires, NCAA materials, and nonathletics recruiting publications.
- You may begin receiving recruiting materials June 15 after your sophomore year.

TELEPHONE CALLS:
- You may make calls to the coach at your expense only.
- College coach can make unlimited calls beginning June 15 after your sophomore year.

OFF-CAMPUS CONTACT: None allowed.
OFFICIAL VISIT: None allowed.
UNOFFICIAL VISIT: You may make an unlimited number of unofficial visits, except during a dead period.

NCAA RECRUIT TIPS: 7 STEPS TO A SCHOLARSHIP

JUNIOR YEAR - DIVISION I
ELECTRONIC CORRESPONDENCE: (text messaging, instant messenger, email)
- You may begin receiving electronic correspondence June 15 after your sophomore year.
- Correspondence must be private between you and the coach until you provide a written commitment to the NCAA school.

RECRUITING MATERIALS:
- Allowed.
- You may begin receiving recruiting materials June 15 after your sophomore year.

TELEPHONE CALLS: You may make calls to the coach at your expense.
COLLEGE COACHES MAY CALL YOU: Unlimited.
OFF-CAMPUS CONTACT:
- Allowed beginning opening day of classes. Contacts other than April period may only occur at your school. Contacts in April may occur at your school or residence.
- No contact on the day of a competition.
- Contacts may not occur during the time of day when classes are in session.

OFFICIAL VISIT:
- Allowed January 1 of your junior year.
- You may make only one official visit per college and up to a maximum of five official visits to Division I colleges. There is no limit to official visits to Division II colleges.

UNOFFICIAL VISIT: You may make an unlimited number of unofficial visits, except during a dead period.

SENIOR YEAR - DIVISION I
ELECTRONIC CORRESPONDENCE:
- You may begin receiving electronic correspondence June 15 after your sophomore year.
- Correspondence must be private between you and the coach until you provide a written commitment to the NCAA school.

RECRUITING MATERIALS: Allowed.
TELEPHONE CALLS: You may make calls to the coach at your expense.
COLLEGE COACHES MAY CALL YOU: Unlimited.
OFF-CAMPUS CONTACT: Allowed.
OFFICIAL VISIT: You may make only one official visit per college and up to a maximum of five official visits to Division I colleges. There is no limit to official visits to Division II colleges.
UNOFFICIAL VISIT: You may make an unlimited number of unofficial visits, except during a dead period.
HOW OFTEN CAN A COACH SEE MEO R TALK TO ME OFF THE COLLEGE'S CAMPUS?
- A college coach may contact you or your parents/legal guardians (including evaluating you off the college's campus) seven times.
- Unlimited number of contacts and evaluation after you sign an NLI, written offer of admission and/or financial aid; OR after the college receives a financial deposit from you.

ALL YEARS - DIVISION II
RECRUITING MATERIALS:
- You may receive brochures for camps, questionnaires, NCAA materials, and nonathletics recruiting publications at any time.
- A coach may begin sending you printed recruiting materials June 15 before your junior year in high school.

TELEPHONE CALLS:
- No limit on number of calls by college coach beginning June 15 before your junior year.
- You may make calls to the coach at your expense.

OFF-CAMPUS CONTACT:
- A college coach can have contact with you or your parents/legal guardians off the college's campus beginning June 15 before your junior year.
- No limit on number of contacts off campus.

UNOFFICIAL VISIT: You may make an unlimited number of unofficial visits any time, except during a dead period.

OFFICIAL VISIT:
- You may make official visits starting June 15 before your junior year.
- You may make only one official visit per college and up to a maximum of five official visits to Division I colleges. There is no limit to official visits to Division II colleges.

ALL YEARS - DIVISION III
RECRUITING MATERIALS: You may receive printed materials any time.

TELEPHONE CALLS:
- No limit on number of calls or when they can be made by the college coach.
- You may make calls to the coach at your expense.

OFF-CAMPUS CONTACT:
- A college coach may begin to have contact with you or your relatives or guardians off the college's campus after your sophomore year.
- No limit on number of off-campus contacts.

UNOFFICIAL VISIT: You may make an unlimited number of unofficial visits any time.

OFFICIAL VISIT:
- You may make official visits starting January 1 of your junior year.
- You may make only one official visit per college and up to a maximum of five official visits to Division I colleges. There is no limit to official visits to Division III colleges.

NCAA RECRUIT TIPS: 7 STEPS TO A SCHOLARSHIP

ALL YEARS - NAIA
RECRUITING MATERIALS:
- You can receive recruiting materials at any time (FR/SO/JR/SR) from NAIA coaches

TELEPHONE CALLS:
- NAIA coaches can make recruiting calls at any time (FR/SO/JR/SR) to recruits

ON-CAMPUS TRYOUTS:
- Students are permitted a maximum of two days of NAIA tryouts throughout their entire career, and the tryout cannot interfere with school time. The NAIA tryout must occur on campus. If a school has a policy for reimbursing all students for such visits, the same can be applied to you as a prospective student-athlete.

VISITS:
- There are no limits on the number of NAIA schools that prospects are allowed to visit, although most do not offer Official Visits.

WOMEN'S BASKETBALL

SOPHOMORE YEAR - DIVISION I
RECRUITING MATERIALS: You may receive brochures for camps, questionnaires, NCAA materials, and nonathletics recruiting publications.
TELEPHONE CALLS:
- You may make calls to the coach at your expense only.
- College coach cannot call you

OFF-CAMPUS CONTACT: None allowed.
OFFICIAL VISIT: None allowed.
UNOFFICIAL VISIT: You may make an unlimited number of unofficial visits, except during a dead period.

JUNIOR YEAR - DIVISION I
ELECTRONIC CORRESPONDENCE (text messaging, instant messenger, email)
- You may begin receiving electronic correspondence September 1 of your junior year.
- Correspondence must be private between you and the coach until you provide a written commitment to the NCAA school.

RECRUITING MATERIALS: You may begin receiving September 1 of your junior year.
TELEPHONE CALLS: You may make calls to the coach at your expense.
COLLEGE COACHES MAY CALL YOU: Unlimited beginning September 1 of your junior year.
OFF-CAMPUS CONTACT
- Allowed September 1 at the beginning of your junior year.
- No contact on the day of a competition.

OFFICIAL VISIT
- Allowed April of your junior year beginning Thursday following the Women's Final Four.

UNOFFICIAL VISIT: You may make an unlimited number of unofficial visits, except during a dead period.

SENIOR YEAR - DIVISION I
ELECTRONIC CORRESPONDENCE:
- You may begin receiving electronic correspondence September 1 of your junior year.
- Correspondence must be private between you and the coach until you provide a written commitment to the NCAA school.

RECRUITING MATERIALS: Allowed.
TELEPHONE CALLS: You may make calls to the coach at your expense.
COLLEGE COACHES MAY CALL YOU: Unlimited.
OFF-CAMPUS CONTACT: Allowed.
OFFICIAL VISIT: You may make only one official visit per college and up to a maximum of five official visits to Division I colleges. There is no limit to official visits to Division II colleges.
UNOFFICIAL VISIT : You may make an unlimited number of unofficial visits, except during a dead period.
HOW OFTEN CAN A COACH SEE ME OR TALK TO ME OFF THE COLLEGE'S CAMPUS?
- A college coach may contact you or your parents/legal guardians (including evaluating you off the college's campus) seven times.
- Unlimited number of contacts and evaluation after you sign an NLI, written offer of admission and/or financial aid; OR after the college receives a financial deposit from you.

ALL YEARS - DIVISION II
RECRUITING MATERIALS
- You may receive brochures for camps, questionnaires, NCAA materials, and nonathletics recruiting publications at any time.
- A coach may begin sending you printed recruiting materials June 15 before your junior year in high school.

TELEPHONE CALLS
- No limit on number of calls by college coach beginning June 15 before your junior year.
- You may make calls to the coach at your expense.

OFF-CAMPUS CONTACT
- A college coach can have contact with you or your parents/legal guardians off the college's campus beginning June 15 before your junior year.
- No limit on number of contacts off campus.

UNOFFICIAL VISIT: You may make an unlimited number of unofficial visits any time, except during a dead period.
OFFICIAL VISIT
- You may make official visits starting June 15 before your junior year.
- You may make only one official visit per college and up to a maximum of five official visits to Division I colleges. There is no limit to official visits to Division II colleges.

NCAA RECRUIT TIPS: 7 STEPS TO A SCHOLARSHIP

ALL YEARS - DIVISION III
RECUITING MATERIALS: You may receive printed materials any time.
TELEPHONE CALLS
- No limit on number of calls or when they can be made by the college coach.
- You may make calls to the coach at your expense.

OFF-CAMPUS CONTACT
- A college coach may begin to have contact with you or your relatives or guardians off the college's campus after your sophomore year.
- No limit on number of off-campus contacts.

UNOFFICIAL VISIT: You may make an unlimited number of unofficial visits any time.
OFFICIAL VISIT
- You may make official visits starting January 1 of your junior year.
- You may make only one official visit per college and up to a maximum of five official visits to Division I colleges. There is no limit to official visits to Division III colleges.

ALL YEARS - NAIA
RECRUITING MATERIALS:
- You can receive recruiting materials at any time (FR/SO/JR/SR) from NAIA coaches

TELEPHONE CALLS:
- NAIA coaches can make recruiting calls at any time (FR/SO/JR/SR) to recruits

ON-CAMPUS TRYOUTS:
- Students are permitted a maximum of two days of NAIA tryouts throughout their entire career, and the tryout cannot interfere with school time. The NAIA tryout must occur on campus. If a school has a policy for reimbursing all students for such visits, the same can be applied to you as a prospective student-athlete.

VISITS:
- There are no limits on the number of NAIA schools that prospects are allowed to visit, although most do not offer Official Visits.

FOOTBALL
SOPHOMORE YEAR - DIVISION I
RECRUITING MATERIALS
- You may receive brochures for camps, questionnaires, NCAA materials, and nonathletics recruiting publications.

TELEPHONE CALLS
- You may make calls to the coach at your expense only.
- College coach cannot call you.

OFF-CAMPUS CONTACT: None allowed.
OFFICIAL VISIT: None allowed.
UNOFFICIAL VISIT: You may make an unlimited number of unofficial visits, except during a dead period.

JUNIOR YEAR - DIVISION I
ELECTRONIC CORRESPONDENCE (text messaging, instant messenger, email)
- Email and fax permissible September 1 of your junior year. All other forms of electronic correspondence is impermissible.
- All forms of electronic correspondence are permissible after you provide a written commitment to the NCAA school.

RECRUITING MATERIALS: You may begin receiving September 1 of your junior year.
TELEPHONE CALLS: You may make calls to the coach at your expense.
COLLEGE COACHES MAY CALL YOU: One call from April 15 to May 31 of your junior year. Additional calls may not be made before September 1 of your senior year.
OFF-CAMPUS CONTACT: None allowed.
OFFICIAL VISIT: None allowed.
UNOFFICIAL VISIT: You may make an unlimited number of unofficial visits, except during a dead period.

SENIOR YEAR - DIVISION I
ELECTRONIC CORRESPONDENCE
- All forms of electronic correspondence (e.g., texting) may be sent to a student-athlete beginning September 1 of your junior year.

RECRUITING MATERIALS: Allowed.
TELEPHONE CALLS: You may make calls to the coach at your expense.
COLLEGE COACHES MAY CALL YOU
- Once per week beginning September 1 outside contact period.
- Unlimited calls after you sign an NLI, written offer of admission and/ or financial aid; OR after the college receives a financial deposit from you.
- Unlimited during contact period.

OFF-CAMPUS CONTACT: Allowed.
OFFICIAL VISIT
- Allowed beginning opening day of classes your senior year.
- You may make only one official visit per college and up to a maximum of five official visits to Division I colleges. There is no limit to official visits to Division II colleges.

UNOFFICIAL VISIT: You may make an unlimited number of unofficial visits, except during a dead period.
HOW OFTEN CAN A COACH SEE ME OR TALK TO ME OFF THE COLLEGE'S CAMPUS?
- A college coach may contact you or your parents/legal guardians (including evaluating you off the college's campus) six times.
- One evaluation during September, October and November.
- Two evaluations— April 15 through May 31 (once to evaluate athletics ability and once to evaluate academic qualifications).
- Unlimited number of contacts and evaluation after you sign an NLI, written offer of admission and/or financial aid; OR after the college receives a financial deposit from you.

NCAA RECRUIT TIPS: 7 STEPS TO A SCHOLARSHIP

ALL YEARS - DIVISION II
RECRUITING MATERIALS:
- You may receive brochures for camps, questionnaires, NCAA materials, and nonathletics recruiting publications at any time.
- A coach may begin sending you printed recruiting materials June 15 before your junior year in high school.

TELEPHONE CALLS:
- No limit on number of calls by college coach beginning June 15 before your junior year.
- You may make calls to the coach at your expense.

OFF-CAMPUS CONTACT:
- A college coach can have contact with you or your parents/legal guardians off the college's campus beginning June 15 before your junior year.
- No limit on number of contacts off campus.

UNOFFICIAL VISIT: You may make an unlimited number of unofficial visits any time, except during a dead period.

OFFICIAL VISIT
- You may make official visits starting June 15 before your junior year.
- You may make only one official visit per college and up to a maximum of five official visits to Division I colleges. There is no limit to official visits to Division II colleges.

ALL YEARS - DIVISION III
RECRUITING MATERIALS: You may receive printed materials any time.

TELEPHONE CALLS
- No limit on number of calls or when they can be made by the college coach.
- You may make calls to the coach at your expense.

OFF-CAMPUS CONTACT
- A college coach may begin to have contact with you or your relatives or guardians off the college's campus after your sophomore year.
- No limit on number of off-campus contacts.

UNOFFICIAL VISIT: You may make an unlimited number of unofficial visits any time.

OFFICIAL VISIT
- You may make official visits starting January 1 of your junior year.
- You may make only one official visit per college and up to a maximum of five official visits to Division I colleges. There is no limit to official visits to Division III colleges.

ALL YEARS - NAIA
RECRUITING MATERIALS:
- You can receive recruiting materials at any time (FR/SO/JR/SR) from NAIA coaches

TELEPHONE CALLS:
- NAIA coaches can make recruiting calls at any time (FR/SO/JR/SR) to recruits

ON-CAMPUS TRYOUTS:
- Students are permitted a maximum of two days of NAIA tryouts throughout their entire career, and the tryout cannot interfere with school time. The NAIA tryout must occur on campus. If a school has a policy for reimbursing all students for such visits, the same can be applied to you as a prospective student-athlete.

VISITS:
- There are no limits on the number of NAIA schools that prospects are allowed to visit, although most do not offer Official Visits.

SPORTS OTHER THAN MBB, WBB AND FOOTBALL

SOPHOMORE YEAR - DIVISION I
RECRUITING MATERIALS:
- You may receive brochures for camps, questionnaires, NCAA materials, and nonathletics recruiting publications.
- Men's Ice Hockey—You may begin receiving recruiting materials January 1 of your sophomore year.

TELEPHONE CALLS:
- You may make calls to the coach at your expense only.
- College coach cannot call you.
- Women's Ice Hockey—A college coach may call international college bound student-athletes once on or after July 7 through July 31 after sophomore year.
- Men's Ice Hockey—May not be made before January 1 of sophomore year.

OFF-CAMPUS CONTACT:
- None allowed.
- Men's Ice Hockey—May not be made before June 15 after sophomore year

OFFICIAL VISIT: None allowed.
UNOFFICIAL VISIT: You may make an unlimited number of unofficial visits, except during a dead period.

JUNIOR YEAR - DIVISION I
ELECTRONIC CORRESPONDENCE: (text messaging, instant messenger, email)
- All forms of electronic correspondence permissible September 1 of your junior year.
- Correspondence must be private until you provide a written commitment to the NCAA school.
- Men's Ice Hockey— You may begin receiving Jan. 1 your sophomore year.

RECRUITING MATERIALS:
- You may begin receiving September 1 of your junior year.
- Men's Ice Hockey— You may begin receiving recruiting materials January 1 after your sophomore year.

TELEPHONE CALLS: You may make calls to the coach at your expense.
COLLEGE COACHES MAY CALL YOU:
- May not be made before Sept. 1 at the beginning of your junior year.

NCAA RECRUIT TIPS: 7 STEPS TO A SCHOLARSHIP

- Women's Ice Hockey—Once per week beginning July 7 after your junior year.
- Swimming & Diving— Beginning July 1 prior to your junior year.
- Cross Country and Track & Field— Beginning July 1 after your junior year

OFF-CAMPUS CONTACT:
- Allowed starting July 1 after your junior year.
- Women's Gymnastics—Allowed beginning July 15 after your junior year.
- Women's Ice Hockey—Allowed beginning July 7 after your junior year.

OFFICIAL VISIT: None allowed.

UNOFFICIAL VISIT: You may make an unlimited number of unofficial visits, except during a dead period.

SENIOR YEAR - DIVISION I

ELECTRONIC CORRESPONDENCE:
- All forms of electronic correspondence permissible September 1 of your junior year.
- Correspondence must be private until you provide a written commitment to the NCAA school.

RECRUITING MATERIALS: Allowed.

TELEPHONE CALLS: You may make calls to the coach at your expense.

COLLEGE COACHES MAY CALL YOU
- Women's Ice Hockey —Once per week beginning July 7 after your junior year.
- Unlimited calls after you sign an NLI, written offer of admission and/ or financial aid; OR after the college receives a financial deposit from you.

OFF-CAMPUS CONTACT: Allowed.

OFFICIAL VISIT
- Allowed beginning opening day of classes your senior year.
- You may make only one official visit per college and up to a maximum of five official visits to Division I colleges. There is no limit to official visits to Division II colleges.

UNOFFICIAL VISIT: You may make an unlimited number of unofficial visits, except during a dead period.

HOW OFTEN CAN A COACH SEE ME OR TALK TO ME OFF THE COLLEGE'S CAMPUS?
- A college coach may contact you or your parents/legal guardians not more than three times.
- Unlimited number of contacts and evaluation after you sign an NLI, written offer of admission and/or financial aid; OR after the college receives a financial deposit from you.

ALL YEARS - DIVISION II

RECRUITING MATERIALS:
- You may receive brochures for camps, questionnaires, NCAA materials, and nonathletics recruiting publications at any time.
- A coach may begin sending you printed recruiting materials June 15 before your junior year in high school.

TELEPHONE CALLS:
- No limit on number of calls by college coach beginning June 15 before your junior year.
- You may make calls to the coach at your expense.

OFF-CAMPUS CONTACT:

- A college coach can have contact with you or your parents/legal guardians off the college's campus beginning June 15 before your junior year.
- No limit on number of contacts off campus.

UNOFFICIAL VISIT: You may make an unlimited number of unofficial visits any time, except during a dead period.

OFFICIAL VISIT:
- You may make official visits starting June 15 before your junior year.
- You may make only one official visit per college and up to a maximum of five official visits to Division I colleges. There is no limit to official visits to Division II colleges.

ALL YEARS - DIVISION III

RECRUITING MATERIALS: You may receive printed materials any time.

TELEPHONE CALLS:
- No limit on number of calls or when they can be made by the college coach.
- You may make calls to the coach at your expense.

OFF-CAMPUS CONTACT:
- A college coach may begin to have contact with you or your relatives or guardians off the college's campus after your sophomore year.
- No limit on number of off-campus contacts.

UNOFFICIAL VISIT: You may make an unlimited number of unofficial visits any time.

OFFICIAL VISIT:
- You may make official visits starting January 1 of your junior year.
- You may make only one official visit per college and up to a maximum of five official visits to Division I colleges. There is no limit to official visits to Division III colleges.

ALL YEARS - NAIA

RECRUITING MATERIALS:
- You can receive recruiting materials at any time (FR/SO/JR/SR) from NAIA coaches

TELEPHONE CALLS:
- NAIA coaches can make recruiting calls at any time (FR/SO/JR/SR) to recruits

ON-CAMPUS TRYOUTS:
- Students are permitted a maximum of two days of NAIA tryouts throughout their entire career, and the tryout cannot interfere with school time. The NAIA tryout must occur on campus. If a school has a policy for reimbursing all students for such visits, the same can be applied to you as a prospective student-athlete.

VISITS:
- There are no limits on the number of NAIA schools that prospects are allowed to visit, although most do not offer Official Visits.

BEFORE THE SCHOLARSHIP OFFER, 20 SIGNS THAT A COLLEGE COACH IS INTERESTED IN YOU

Below are 20 signs that a college coach is interested in recruiting you. Depending on their interest level, their actions will vary. Remember, depending on your age, there are limits on to how coaches can recruit you and what type of contact they can have with you.

<u>1-5 signs</u>: Low-Mid level of interest
<u>5-10 signs</u>: Mid-High level of interest
<u>10 or more signs</u>: Coaches are highly interested in you and considering you for a scholarship

#1- Sent you a questionnaire

#2- Send you mail and/or emails. Handwritten letters and cards show a higher level of interest.

#3- Call you. The more they call you (as allowed), the more interested they are.

#4- Call your family and coaches to get to know them, and to get to know more about you.

#5- Invite you to camp

#6- Follow or friend request you on social media

#7- Request film from your coaches

#8- Invite you to campus for a game, Junior Day, tour, unofficial visit

#9- Encourage you to register for the NCAA Eligibility Center and to register for the ACT/SAT tests

#10- Come to your school, games, practice or tournaments. The more often that they show up, the more interest they have. Best case scenario: the head coach shows up at your games! Great sign if multiple coaches from that school come to your school or games, they are cross-checking their evaluations and discussing you as a staff.

#11- Request your high school transcript

#12- Ask you questions and gauge your interest in their program

YOUR COACHES WANT NOTHING MORE THAN TO TRUST YOU, NO MATTER WHAT YOU THINK! THEY WANT YOU TO BREAK OUT AND SUCCEED!

#13- Send you info on the specific major that you are interested in

#14- Are asking around about you... Your coaches, rival coaches, teachers, principal, guidance counselors, etc. They are trying to get the full picture about you as a player, student and person from all angles.

#15- Talk about setting up an official visit down the road. If they begin checking dates with you for a possible Official Visit, they are interested!

#16- Mention making an in-home visit with you and your family down the road. If they bring up a future in-home visit, they're interested!

#17- Tell you to watch their games and get a feel for their style of play. As they get to know you, they want you to get to know them, their philosophy and style as a team and coaching staff.

#18- Ask you personal questions. When coaches are interested in your athletic ability and considering offering you, they will want to get to know you on a personal level and will ask you about hobbies, likes/dislikes, favorites, girlfriends/boyfriends, etc. They will want to get to know more about you as a person!

#19- Ask you which schools have visited you and/or offered you. They will want to know who they are competing against. They will want to know more about your selection factors and how they compare with those other schools. Do they have a good shot with you?

#20- If you are in town and make an unofficial visit, they will take time to take you on a campus and facility tour. If they want to show you what they have to offer about a program, they are interested!

YOUR DECISION TIMELINE
Be very up front with coaches about your timeline, it's a factor they will work to understand and college coaches will often ask you, your prep coaches, your family and those close to you about. Coaches are trying to understand HOW you are planning to do your research and WHEN you are planning on making a decision.

Think about it... do you want to decide early and get all of the drama over before your senior season or do you want to focus on your season first and then decide after you are done playing? If you are an elite player, most schools will wait as long as you need if they are THAT interested. Some schools may let you know that they have to move on if you haven't decided by a specific deadline. No matter what your timeline is, it's best to be

LEARN WHAT IT MEANS TO BE RELENTLESS:

'I WILL NOT BE DENIED.'

open and honest with the coaches who are recruiting you about your timeline and when you plan to make a decision to commit.

Most coaches will keep it real with you about how long they are willing to wait if you keep it real with them about your timeline and how you want to handle the process. If you don't tell them directly, they'll definitely be asking everyone around you, and those people may not be able to give them the correct answer. They just want to understand you and it's always best if they hear that information directly from you.

On a few occasions, I've worked with coaches who held out for better players and were rejected just days before Signing Day—or at the end of the actual day! That opened the door for one or two other recruits who got the offer after a year or more of waiting. If you are in this situation, you are going to have to be very patient and understand that that offer may never come. It's important that you understand the system and make the best decision possible for you based on your preferences. You may be waiting for that date with a supermodel, and that call may never come. Don't let the great school-next-door get away!

THE WOO-ING STAGE

If you are the #1 player a coach wants, they will trip over themselves to make an impression with you and those close to you. They will call, write, fax, Facebook, Skype, tweet, show up and your games... anything to show you that you are their first choice and always in their plans. Some of the best recruiters have a sense of confidence about themselves and are very direct about the fact that they're willing to do anything to chase you down and prove to you that you belong on their campus!

All great recruiters know this—they just need a CHANCE. If you are their top priority and they work relentlessly to recruit you they may get the chance to be in your Top 5. After that, they want the chance to work their way into your Top 3 and maybe even be the school that signs you. Most good recruiters have the first critical goal of just getting you to campus for a visit or a game. To a lot of recruiters, that's their #1 goal. They may feel that if they can get you to their house and can show you what they have to offer, then they've got a shot!

CLOSING THE DEAL ON HOME TURF

There are two important events that take place in the recruiting process, both revolving around that 'at home' feeling— Official/Unofficial Visits and in-home visits. To recruiters, there is no place like home!

I will go into depth on page 113 about the questions you need to get answers to during the recruiting process and during Official and Unofficial Visits, remember that it's very important to get to the campus of the school that you are thinking about committing to before you make your decision. It's best that you go there in person to know what you're getting yourself into— the coaches, the campus, the students, the gameday atmosphere, the city, the dorms... everything! Ideally, you don't want to commit to a university until you've gotten a chance to get to their place and can see how they live!

Compare it to online dating, everyone posts their most flattering pictures, writes great profiles and most times they aren't 100% accurate. Old pictures, exaggerations, their personality is rarely what was portrayed in their 'About Me' section. You wouldn't shop for a spouse on the internet and agree to get married without meeting them! Same for every college program that you are considering— it's very important to see them for your own two eyes before signing anything or committing!

There is always a chance that you may not feel comfortable in the community, with the campus, with the personality of the team or in your situation after meeting with the coaches in person, on campus.

A great sign of interest from a coach is when they're inviting you to campus for an official or unofficial visit. If they're inviting you to their games, Junior Days, other campus events or games—they're interested on some level and what to get to know you better.

Throughout the recruiting process, understand that it's a two-way street. Coaches are constantly evaluating if you are a good fit for their program but THEY also want YOU to do your research, kick in the tires and go for a test drive. They want you to feel a fit with them and know that won't truly happen until you've been to their campus. You need to be evaluating them just as carefully as they are evaluating you!

When coaches are ready to close the deal they will usually make the trip to your hometown for an in-home visit. They want to be on your turf, show you that they can fit in with your family and can tell you what their plan is for you. They have been selling to you but this is a final chance to close the deal with those close to you who may also be influencing your decision.

The highest sign of interest that coaches can show you is by getting you to their house for an official visit and getting the opportunity to come to yours for an in-home visit. They will be trying to close the deal on both turfs!

PRESSURE-TIME TO COMMIT
Once a coach has scouted you, offered you, had you to campus for an official or unofficial visit there will probably come a time when they will begin to put the pressure on you to commit. The goal of every recruiting cycle is to sign the best player to each available scholarship. This phase is a lot like the weeks before Homecoming... when every guy is trying to convince the prettiest girl in school to go to the dance with them. Every coaching staff

wants their #1 choice to say yes and to end any speculation about them having interest in any other school.

Each staff sits down and determines their needs by position for the next few years – where will the team be in one or two years? What spots will be open or what positions do they need depth at?

Coaches don't begin this process the summer before your senior year, they begin it during your freshman and sophomore years!

Coaches first look at their roster – our QB will be a senior in two years, are we comfortable with the next guy in line and who will be the backup to him? What positions need better depth? What if someone gets injured? Is there a chance that our freshman center will go to the NBA after next season? Three projected starters on our offensive line will be seniors in two years, who will be in the system by that time and are they ready to lead? Since predicting the future is impossible, all coaches can do is make several projections and base their recruiting needs from there. Normally they put priority on certain positions and little or no priority on others, just depending on who is already on the roster or signed for next two or three seasons.

Once a coach has zeroed in on you and started building those relationships with your inner circle, is getting positive feedback on your interest in the program, there comes a time when they'll start putting some sort of pressure on you to commit. They want to lock you up and focus on the next priority on their list. They'll still continue to communicate with you and recruit you (call you and come to your games) but they'll also want to shift their focus on getting a commitment from the next biggest position need.

I'M CHALLENGING YOU TO TURN YOUR BIGGEST WEAKNESS INTO A STRENGTH! OVERCOMING THAT INSECURITY IS KEY TO GAINING CONFIDENCE.

As you get deeper in the recruiting process, dominos start falling... similar to the time leading up to the Homecoming. Coaches have a ranked list by position of their needs and wants. Their #1 WR, #2 WR, #3 WR and so on... like the prettiest girls in school. There will come a time when players around the country (or state) start committing and there's a scramble to put the pressure on the best available players. A school may have ranked the top WR target for their system, but if they're getting little positive communication back, and if they know that player is listening to many other pitches, they may go for the 'definite' player who may be a little lower on their list but who will be more likely to commit. Coaches ask, "Who is the BEST player that we can REALISTICALLY get and how long can we wait on our top targets?"

There are some cases when coaches will hang on to an extra scholarship until Signing Day or later for a big-time player for their program. Big name programs know that they can hold out until the last minute for that star recruit, and if they are rejected they can still find a great player that will accept the offer down the road. I've worked with some coaches who hang on to scholarships until they are 100% sure of a player.

Everyone wants to go to the dance with the best option—who will say yes—so if coaches aren't getting the vibe that they have a realistic shot with you, they may move on to the next-best player available.

You might not have much of a warning, so don't play coy. If you are interested, be up front about it. If you are unsure, tell the coach you are still doing your research. If you are in love with them, let them know before they move on to somebody else!

14 SIGNS OF A GREAT RECRUITER

Before you get too deep in the recruiting process it's important for you to learn the difference between what it takes to be a great recruiter and what to look for in a great coach.

Recruiting players and coaching players are two completely different jobs – and not too many people understand that. Recruiting and coaching require different skill sets. Just become someone is a great recruiter, it doesn't necessarily mean they are a great coach. And there are really great coaches who may not naturally be great at recruiting players.

During the recruiting process, you are only really seeing one side of a coach. Recruiting has become such a critical role in a coach's job description because it has become so competitive nationally, but it's only one-third of their job.

NCAA RECRUIT TIPS: 7 STEPS TO A SCHOLARSHIP

Characteristics of great recruiters include:

#1: A genuine-seeming personality

#2: A master of marketing – 24/7/365

#3: A high-level of organization and attention to detail

#4: A coach who is diligent in their work ethic

#5: The ability to put on a show

#6: The ability to get to know who or what is important in your life and to keep up with what is going on in your world

#7: The ability to create a parent role in your life

#8: The effort of getting to know all of the decision makers and influencers in your life (prep coaches, parents, extended family, mentors, girlfriends/boyfriends)

#9: A confidence about their program, what they can offer you and their ability to get you to commit

#10: The ability to be able to move on to the next player if they aren't getting feedback or interest from their top prospects

#11: Putting together an official visit weekend that will be a home run from your perspective, creating the vision that you have told them that you are looking for in a program

#12: The ability to do skill evaluations without solely relying on rankings or scouting reports

#13: The ability to determine position needs for the team and sign the best available player at that position

#14: Having strong relationships with coaches and programs in their region
Remember—throughout the process you are ultimately looking for a coach who is a great TEACHER. The ability to recruit players helps coaches get and keep their jobs, but the ability to TEACH players is what you are ultimately looking for! Know the difference!

@1001RecruitTips

ACTION STEPS: UNDERSTAND HOW COACHES EVALUATE PLAYERS AND BUILD THEIR SIGNING CLASSES

- **FIGURE OUT WHICH COACHES RECRUIT YOUR SCHOOL/POSITION AT UNIVERSITIES YOU ARE INTERESTED IN:** AS YOU BEGIN TO FIGURE OUT WHICH LEVEL OF COMPETITION YOU ARE BEING RECRUITED IT, BEGIN REACHING OUT TO OTHER COACHES AT THOSE LEVELS (AND THE LIST YOU WILL DEVELOP ON PAGE 60). BEGIN CONTACTING EACH SCHOOL OR DO YOUR RESEARCH ONLINE TO FIND OUT WHICH COACH RECRUITS YOUR HIGH SCHOOL, POSITION OR GRADE (SEE PAGE 52).

- **FUNDAMENTALS FIRST:** WHAT ARE THE TOP FEW FUNDAMENTALS OF YOUR POSITION - OR THE POSITIONS YOU WOULD LIKE TO BE RECRUITED AT? WORK DAILY ON IMPROVING THOSE FUNDAMENTALS! REMEMBER, COACHES ARE LOOKING FOR PLAYERS WHO ARE PHENOMENAL AT THE BASICS! DON'T FOCUS ON THE FLASH, FOCUS ON THE FUNDAMENTALS! AS A FRESHMAN OR SOPHOMORE, IT'S BEST TO SPEND TIME DEVELOPING THESE BASICS INSTEAD OF TRYING TO CHASE THE EARLY RECRUITING ATTENTION!

FUNDAMENTALS TO FOCUS ON IMPROVING:
_____
_____
_____

- **KEEP UP WITH YOUR ACADEMICS:** I'VE WORKED WITH SEVERAL COACHES WHO HAVE PULLED SCHOLARSHIP OFFERS BECAUSE PLAYERS WHO HAVE COMMITTED THOUGHT THEY COULD DROP THEIR SCHOOL WORK SINCE THEY HAD ALREADY MADE A COMMITMENT. CONTINUE TO HANDLE YOUR BUSINESS IN THE CLASSROOM, SET TIME ASIDE TO STUDY AND DO HOMEWORK AND BE PREPARED. COACHES WILL BE ASKING FOR FEEDBACK FROM YOUR TEACHERS OF HOW YOU HANDLE CLASSES, EVEN AFTER YOU HAVE COMMITTED! NOTHING IMPRESSES COACHES MORE THAN WHEN PLAYERS FINISH STRONG!

- **UNDERSTAND HOW AND WHEN COACHES CAN CONTACT YOU:** NCAA RULES REGULATE WHEN AND HOW OFTEN COLLEGE COACHES CAN CONTACT YOU, BUT THERE AREN'T ANY RULES ABOUT WHEN YOU ARE ABLE TO CONTACT THEM! UNDERSTAND THAT IF YOU AREN'T HEARING FROM, OR HEARING BACK FROM COLLEGE COACHES, IT MAY BE BECAUSE OF YOUR AGE -- THEY AREN'T ALLOWED TO RESPOND TO EMAILS, TEXTS OR VOICEMAILS UNTIL AFTER CERTAIN TIMES OF YOUR HIGH SCHOOL CAREER (SEE PAGE 88-98).

COACHES OF MY SPORT CAN BEGIN CONTACTING ME:
_____

NCAA RECRUIT TIPS: 7 STEPS TO A SCHOLARSHIP

- **GET TO KNOW COACHES PERSONALLY:** COACHES PUT A LOT OF TIME INTO TRYING TO FIGURE OUT WHO YOU ARE AS A PERSON. YOU NEED TO DO THE SAME THING, GET TO KNOW THE COACHES WHO ARE RECRUITING YOU, AND GET TO KNOW THEIR PERSONALITIES OUTSIDE OF JUST SPORTS. DURING THE RECRUITING PROCESS YOU WILL BE GETTING THE SUGAR-COATED, BEST-BEHAVED VERSION OF THEM -- ARE THERE ANY RED FLAGS THAT LEAD YOU TO THINK THEY MAY BE UNTRUSTWORTHY? FOLLOW YOUR GUT WHEN IT COMES TO EVALUATING A COACH'S CHARACTER.

- **UNDERSTAND WHICH PROGRAMS ARE LEGITIMATELY INTERESTED:** EVEN IF YOU ARE GETTING MAIL AND EMAILS FROM COACHES, THAT DOESN'T NECESSARILY MEAN THAT THEY ARE SINCERELY INTERESTED IN YOU (RIGHT NOW). YOU DON'T WANT TO PUT ALL YOUR HOPES AND DREAMS INTO A TINY BIT OF INTEREST YOU MAY BE RECEIVING. GAUGE HOW SERIOUS THE INTEREST IS FROM PROGRAMS THAT YOU ARE HEARING FROM NOW, AND IF YOU FEEL LIKE IT'S JUST EARLY OR VERY LITTLE LEGITIMATE INTEREST, MAKE SURE YOU ARE STARTING TO REACH OUT ON YOUR OWN TO OTHER PROGRAMS.

SCHOOLS THAT ARE SHOWING ME LEGITIMATE INTEREST:

_____

_____

_____

- **YOUR DECISION TIMELINE:** SIT DOWN WITH YOUR FAMILY AND MENTORS TO DECIDE WHAT A GOOD TIMELINE WOULD BE TO COMMIT, ESPECIALLY IF YOU ARE GETTING A LOT OF INTEREST. DO YOU WANT TO COMMIT EARLY IN THE PROCESS, OR BEFORE THE SEASON TO ELIMINATE DISTRACTIONS? OR, WOULD YOU RATHER PUT RECRUITING AND CAMPUS VISITS ON HOLD UNTIL AFTER YOUR PREP SEASON IS OVER? DECIDE WHAT WOULD BE THE BEST SCHEDULE FOR YOU TO KEEP YOUR ACADEMICS, PLAYING SEASON AND MIND STRAIGHT FOR WHAT IS MOST IMPORTANT. IF A COACH IS SINCERELY INTERESTED IN YOU, THEY WILL WAIT IF THEY NEED TO.

I PLAN TO TAKE UNOFFICIAL/OFFICIAL VISITS TO WHICH CAMPUSES WHEN:

_____

_____

_____

_____

_____

@1001RecruitTips

STEP #4
DEVELOPING & NARROWING YOUR LIST

"As children we learn to turn over, to sit up, to crawl, then to walk and run. Each step is important. No step can be skipped."
-STEPHEN R. COVEY

"What you do, it speaks so loudly... it doesn't matter what you say. It doesn't matter what you say, it matters what you do!"
-COACH NICK SABAN

"Every time you have to speak, you are auditioning for leadership."
-JAMES HUMES

NCAA RECRUIT TIPS: 7 STEPS TO A SCHOLARSHIP

DEVELOP YOUR LIST: WHAT'S IMPORTANT TO YOU

Coaches have their own checklist of characteristics and skills that they are looking for. You need to develop one as well! As you sit down, think about the few things that are really important to you, that will help you become a successful player, eventual college graduate and person. In order to be successful in a situation, you need to be happy -- this is why it is so critical to base your decision on these few factors that are really important to you.

Whether it is distance from home, early playing time, a specific major, internship opportunities, path to the pros, etc... put together your short list of needs. What does the final opportunity need to have in order to make you happy and comfortable with the decision.

As the process picks up, coaches will undoubtedly through a million things at you. Factors you had never even thought of! Ultimately, most of those decision factors don't matter -- just the handful of factors that are important to you and your family.

In times of confusion or pressure, lean on those core needs that you initially set out with and those should help lead you to the best decision for you! Focus on what is really important to you at the end of the day, all of those other frivolous things don't really matter!

30 FACTORS THAT RECRUITS CONSIDER WHEN SELECTING A SCHOOL

Players choose schools for a variety of reasons, many recruits focusing on a key three or four factors they must-have when making their decision. Below are a list of 30 factors (some good and some worthless) that players consider when making their decisions:

#1 - Graduation Rates of Athletes

#2 - Class Size

#3 - Academic Support Available for Student-Athletes

#4 - Degree Programs Offered

#5 - The City the University is Located In

#6 - Distance from Home

#7 - Consistent Success of Athletic Department as a Whole

#8 - Athletic Department Budget

#9 - Program on the Rise After Tough Few Years

#10 - Big Name School vs. Small Name School

#11 - Conference and Level of Competition

#12 - Relationship with the Head Coach or Position Coach

#13 - School Spirit

#14 - Style of Play

#15 - Player Improvement / Development

#16 – Academic Prestige

#17 – Campus Traditions

#18 - Playing Time – Opportunity to Start or Be a Major Contributor

#19 - Facilities

#20 - Draft Record

#21 - Crime Rates

#22 - Visibility to Earn National Individual Awards

#23 - Other Signees

#24 - Attractive Student Body

#25 - Post-Season Opportunities

#26 - Personality of Head Coach

#27 - Opportunity to Win a Championship

#28 - Family Atmosphere

#29 - Two-Sport Athlete Opportunities

#30 – Gear / Uniforms

20 SIGNS OF A SUCCESSFUL COLLEGE COACH

#1: They demand perfection in everything that you do, even off-the- field

#2: They understand that winning is the only thing that they will be judged on and can balance game preparations, strategy and player development with other job requirements that don't necessarily effect wins and losses

#3: They learn from every coach they have worked for and keep everything that has been passed down to them

#4: They are good communicators

#5: They aren't caught off guard on or off-the-field

#6: They demand discipline and are building a team that is disciplined within

#7: They can win versus ranked opponents

#8: Their teams fight back when down

#9: They know how to motivate their players

#10: They have faith and passion in their plan, staff and players

#11: They know how to move on after losses and setbacks

#12: Their players are accountable

#13: They are great teachers and are able to simplify the gameplan

#14: They demand that their players respect the program and the honor of being a college athlete

#15: Their practices are tough

#16: They have strong relationships with other coaches across the sport at every level (high school, college and pros)

#17: They expect their players to graduate

#18: They are prepared for the next step before it happens

#19: They enjoy the process

#20: They know how to manage a staff

QUESTIONS TO ASK DURING RECRUITING PROCESS

Whether choosing a school as a blue-chip prospect with 50 scholarship offers or as a Division III non-scholarship athlete, it is very important to develop your personal selection criteria that will help you through the process – and prioritize it based on your non- negotiables and your preferences. Before the process becomes overwhelming, what are the core factors that you need to be happy and successful?

There are four core factors that you need to research:
#1: Academics
#2: Town and University Community
#3: Athletic Department
#4: Your Specific Team/Position

It is each COACH'S' job to sign the best athletes that will put their program in the best position to win. As a staff, they have clearly defined their 'must-haves' in prospective student-athletes at each position. It is YOUR job to define what you need, to do your research and to ask the right questions in order to put yourself in the best position possible to succeed. Don't forget—your job is just as important as their job during the evaluation process!

Determine the handful of core factors that you will be making your decision off of, and stick to evaluating those! Don't get heavily influenced by the other things that truly aren't important to you!

Coaches may be throwing the kitchen sink at you in terms of what they have to offer, but many of those things may not be what is truly important to you in the long run. Don't get distracted!

Take a page from NFL scouts: they ask receptionists, lunch ladies, trainers, coaches, stadium security guards and anyone else a player may come in contact with to find out their true colors—not just how they act around coaches or perform on the field. An NFL prospects 'true colors' are almost as important as their athletic ability when it comes to breaking down the top talent, how is the player mentally, spiritually and what type of person are they? How do they handle success, how do they handle adversity? How do they act behind closed doors or when the cameras are off and when the recruits aren't around? NFL teams are making decisions between one player and another and investing millions and millions of dollars into draft picks—they need to know about every aspect of their life. YOU should take that same consideration with programs and coaches. It's more about what they're not telling you that you need to look into. Do your research!

> **IF YOU ARE TRULY TRYING YOUR HARDEST, NEVER LOSE FAITH IN YOURSELF. JUST BECAUSE THE SHINE AND CROWDS AREN'T THERE (YET), THAT DOESN'T MEAN YOU AREN'T IMPROVING!**

NCAA RECRUIT TIPS: 7 STEPS TO A SCHOLARSHIP

Don't let one bad comment or opinion take a school off your list—a lot of dirty recruiting goes on—but listen to PATTERNS. If more and more people have the same reaction to a coach or a program, good or bad, listen. It won't take long to get a good picture when you ask enough people.

Ask several people who personally know the coaches you are evaluating—ask them who they would like their children to play for? Don't let them influence your decision necessarily, but instead you are looking for a PATTERN!!!

10 MUST-ASK QUESTIONS DURING THE RECRUITING PROCESS AND DURING OFFICIAL/UNOFFICIAL VISITS

#1: What are grad rates of your sport nationally, and how do they compare to the schools that you are looking at? Does that university and your specific team graduate their players? What percentage of that teams' players have graduated in the last 5-10 years?

#2: What are the grad rates for the coaches that you are thinking about playing for? Have they made graduating their players a priority over their career? What percentage of that coaches' players (even if they were at another school) have graduated in the last 5-10 years?

#3: Will distance be a factor—do you want to stay within a certain distance from home or do you specifically want to go far away to school?

#4: At some point, ALL players get frustrated with an adversity they face in their athletic career and the first target of that frustration is often living in a city that they don't like. You will need a balance! Do you like what the town has to offer off-campus—outdoor activities, beaches, arts, concerts, shopping, other sports teams, etc?

#5: Are all of the other teams at that school successful within the conference and in post-season play? Is the Athletic Director and leadership happy being competitive or are they able to provide all teams the resources to win? Do all of the teams win on a consistent level?

#6: How many players AT YOUR POSITION do they plan to sign in your graduating class? How many players at your position have already committed, how many slots are left?

#7: What is the average class size? Check the official admissions information from each university for official stats, not just what the coaches are telling you!

#8: If considering several offers, does the athletic department have the resources (booster money/corporate sponsors) to hire great coaches and provide several competitive advantages in terms of resources and operating budget? Is the team "doing more with less" and expecting championships on a shoestring budget or are they providing the competitive resources needed to win consistently?

#9: What is the head coach's personality? Players often mimic their coaches, are they great people? Do they only care about winning or do they truly put their players first in terms of lessons that they are teaching them and standards they are setting? Are they womanizers, cheaters, excuse makers, mentally/physically abusive, etc? When you are spending time with the current players ask them how the head coach treats them once they are enrolled— surprisingly, they will usually tell you the truth, good or bad.

#10: What is their plan for you? No starting job is ever guaranteed, even if they may promise it during the recruiting process. Ask them for their plan and also evaluate the roster for yourself.

MORE QUESTIONS TO ASK...
ACADEMICS

- What percentage of classes have fewer than 30 students? Fewer than 50 students? What are the class sizes within your intended major?

- Do they offer a major that you are interested in?

- Can you sit in on a class during your visit, particularly in your desired major?

- What are the freshman year credit requirements? What will be your freshman year required classes?

- What is the coach's or department's class attendance policy?

- Do you plan on taking summer school classes and what is the department's policy on summer school?

- Do athletes have required study hall hours? What is the team's policy on required study hall?

- What is a sample daily schedule like during the season and in the off-season?

- Are tutors available? What technology resources are available to student-athletes?

- Does the athletic department or school help with networking or job fairs?

- Has the team or department had any academic scandals within recent years?

- If applicable, are there special accommodations for students with learning disabilities? If so, what do they include?

- Check out what the other players select as majors—do they put student-athletes in "easy" programs? Are several players majoring in "General Studies" or similar programs or are they in tougher majors?

- If you plan on going to grad school, law school or medical school —are you in a program that will help you accomplish your future goals and get into the programs that you are interested in?

- Is the academic program a national leader? Is that something that is important to you or are you more interested in "hands on" opportunities with internships?

- If you are interested in internships, are you in the right city where you may be able to network and find the se positions? Does the school place students in great internships?

- Do major companies recruit students from that university?

THE TOWN/UNIVERSITY COMMUNITY

- Schools are usually either in small towns and have a "college town" feel or are in big cities—are you comfortable? Some big-city people get bored easily in small towns or those from small towns are overwhelmed in big cities—do you like the community you will be living in?

- Are you interested in living in a new place outside of your comfort zone for a few years? Move to big city, move out of big city, major climate change, closer to other family/friends—will you be moving to a city that you've always dreamed of living in?

- There is a good chance that your coach won't be there throughout your entire career (it's the nature of the business)—will you still be happy in that town without the coach you are going to play for?

- If you have a spouse and/or children—how will that play into your decision? Is distance a factor? Will they be moving with you? Can you talk to players at the schools that you are interested that are also married or are parents and see how they are able to manage the transition? Do they offer family housing?

ATHLETIC DEPARTMENT
- What do the other athletes think of the Athletic Director and their interactions with them? Does the Athletic Department have great leadership?

- Is the department improving and always bringing in more resources and improvements? Facilities, technology, new athletic training treatments?

- Are the players respected in the community as positive role models? Do they have a history with legal issues?

- Is the Athletic Department profiting? What is their operating budget and how does it compare to the other schools that you are looking at?

- If the department sponsors several teams, are they stretching the budget really thin or does your team have the resources to succeed and compete within the conference or nationally?

YOUR TEAM
- Is the team on the rise? Is there a strong foundation of quality players already in the system that you can learn from and win with? Are they starting from scratch or are there great pieces already in place?

- Will you have time to develop or will you be thrown into the fire as a freshman and expected to deliver or carry the team?

- What is the record of success of the program in last 5-10 years? If the coaching staff is new, what is their track record of success at previous school s?

- Are there any great leaders or mentors that you can learn from?

- Does the team have the opportunity to be a major upset team, does that excite you? Do they play with exceptional heart and like the underdog role?

- If you are a major football or basketball Division I prospect, does the team charter flights for most of their road games so that you will miss less class time? Do they bring tutors or academic counselors on the road?

- Are there certain traditions that you would like to be a part of at a particular school?

- Are their games televised so that your friends and family can watch you often?

- Is there a path for your team to play for a championship or major post-season opportunity?

- Do you want to be a part of a major regional or national rivalry?

- What does the conference offer in terms of academic prestige, competition, tradition, exposure?

- Is there good attendance at games? Is school spirit important to you?

- Is the stadium close to campus? Is it a place you've dreamed of playing?

- Are the teams disciplined on the field or do they make stupid mistakes? Are they undisciplined off-the field with arrests, suspensions or scandals?

- Are the players accountable to each other and competitive? Do they have a positive attitude, work ethic and desire to get better?

- Can you help recruit a 'super class' of other recruits who can come in and make a difference, especially at an underdog team?

- What are the dining halls like? Do they have nutritionists who will help you with nutrition, vitamins, supplements, etc?

YOUR POSITION

- Are you willing to sacrifice playing time at a smaller school to be able to join a high-major team? Or vice versa?

- How is your relationship with your position coach, coordinator or assistant coaches? They will be your primary teachers in many cases, do you get along and believe in their philosophy? Are they coaches you would love to play for?

- Will you be challenged at that school to become the best player that you can become?

- What is the plan for your development?

- Can you test yourself versus the best competition possible, will you get better?

- How are they as COACHES and teachers? Are their players fundamentally sound? How have their players improved over the years, what results can they show you? Watch film with coaches and see what suggestions they have on how you can improve?

- What strength and conditioning improvements would they like to see you make? What is the ideal weight and speed they would like you at, and what weightroom goals would they like to see you at? How have their players improved in terms of strength, speed and conditioning? Do they get pushed around during games?

- How do you fit in to their system and style of play? Is your position underutilized in their system?

WHAT DOESN'T REALLY MATTER
- Are they the biggest, shiniest facilities? (They won't directly help you win, just maybe help recruiting more players.)

- If you go there, will you have a better chance of getting drafted? (Scouts will go anywhere to find the best players, and the cross the country looking for talent. Playing for particular coaches may help you become more fundamentally sound, develop a championship mentality but more of the impact of your coach, not your logo!)

- Can they help you win a national award like the Heisman, Doak, the Naismith, etc? (No school can help you win!)

WHAT TO EXPECT ON UNOFFICIAL /OFFICIAL VISITS
On Official and Unofficial visits, coaches are trying to both get to know you better and let you get a better understanding of them. It's a two-way street and visits are their opportunities to show you what they have to offer.

The important takeaway from visits is getting a feel for what it will be like to live there, go to school there, be among the type of players they have and learn from that coaching staff. Do you feel comfortable? Can you get better? Will you be happy? Are you too far or too close to home?

COMPETITORS: STAY READY FOR YOUR GOLDEN OPPORTUNITY, IT WILL COME!

Unofficial visits are usually a little less personal, depending on where you rank at your position for that staff. For Junior Days and gamedays, some coaching staffs invite hundreds of players who are early in the recruiting cycle, especially if the staff is new and trying to get to know the local and regional players better. Unofficial visits can also be very personalized with just one or two players spending the day with the staff, it varies.

If coaches have interest in you, they will definitely try to get you to visit campus so they can meet you in person or spend more time with you on a personal level. How much personal times they spend with you, and how detailed the visit in can tell you a lot about where you rank on their priority list.

Another key difference is if you scheduled the visit yourself or if you were invited. Not all staffs will take the time, or have the time, to spend with you if you just show up or try to set up a visit on your own. They may also be restricted from meeting with you if you stop by during an NCAA Dead Period.

NCAA RECRUIT TIPS: 7 STEPS TO A SCHOLARSHIP

I'm not saying this to discourage you, I've worked with plenty of players who called and express interest in coming to campus for an Unofficial Visit and who eventually earned scholarship offers—it just really depends on where the coaching staff is in terms of evaluations of your signing class.

If you are invited and coaches spend personal time with you, they have some level of interest in you and are evaluating you for a scholarship.

Another telling sign if the amount of personal time you get with the head coach. If the head coach meets with you one-on-one, that means you are a high priority to them and they are close to offering you. If the head coach spends time with you or pulls you away from the group of prospects, that's a good sign.

<u>**On visits, you may**</u>:

- **Meet with:**
    - Head Coach
    - Offensive/Defensive Coordinator
    - Assistant Coaches
    - Academic Advisors
    - Professor in the major you are interested in
    - Dean of the School you are interested in
    - University President
    - Athletic Director
    - Strength Coach
    - Athletic Trainer
    - Sports Information Director
    - Other coaches on the staff
    - Players at your position or side of the ball
    - Players from your hometown

- **Go on a campus tour to see:**
    - Dorms
    - Classrooms
    - Dining Hall
    - Student Union
    - Lockerroom
    - Athletic Facilities
    - Popular campus spots

- **Game Invites:** If you are being evaluated for a scholarship, coaches will definitely try to get you to come to a game and they will ask you personally. Sure, schools may invite more recruits to games than others, each staff varies... but if you are being invited personally by phone or in person, that's a great sign.

- Watch practice

Understand all visits are choreographed so you will see what they want you to see – and they will keep you away from what they don't want you to see! The people you interact with are hand selected, so understand most coaching staffs are trying to paint a picture of the place you have told them you want to be.

SETTING UP AN UNOFFICIAL VISIT TO A SCHOOL THAT HAS NOT SHOWN INTEREST YET

The good news is within all programs – not all recruits who were offered scholarships were players who the coaches went after and found on their own. A good chunk of players who earn scholarship offers are ones who approached the school first. So, if you aren't gaining much interest and/or if there are some programs you are very interested in but haven't heard from yet, go ahead and reach out on your own!

But it's important to understand that Unofficial Visits, especially ones where coaches devote any significant time to spend with you, are set up if there is mutual interest only.

Sure, sometimes you can call a week in advance and ask for a tour of the facilities and try to set up a meeting with one of the coaches. Some coaches may have time, most may not, if you aren't a player they already know who would be a fit for their program. (If you have no scholarship offers, don't waste your time reaching out to Top 25 teams, trying to set up visits. It's best to start with smaller schools within your area, and working your way up.)

Some programs are more accommodating and can have a grad assistant give you a tour, most may not have the time. Time is priceless to coaches and unless they've seen/heard great things about you already from scouting services or local coaches, seen your game video or highlights or unless you have great size and measureables – you may not get more than a friendly intro... and an invitation to send your video.

DID YOU KNOW... SUPER BOWL MVP AARON RODGERS HAD ZERO DIVISION I SCHOLARSHIP OFFERS COMING OUT OF HIGH SCHOOL

It's best not to just drop in—definitely call a few days or a week in advance before you make the trip all the way there. You may get there and visit during a Dead Period – an NCAA-regulated time when coaches are unable to have contact with prospects on the college campus. You may get there and nobody is available to meet – you definitely need to set up an appointment in advance if you are serious.

KEEP DETAILED NOTES: WRITE THOUGHTS IN THE MOMENT

As you take Unofficial Visits, Official Visits and spend countless hours talking with coaches on the phone, it's easy for your thoughts and impressions to begin to blend together weeks later once you're home. A great practice is keep a notebook, with space for each school or coach to have their own section for notes. Keep track of what was discussed during the conversations, how you feel about the coaching staff, what the players are like, notes about the academic programs, your first impressions of the campus and University city while they're fresh in your mind and any other feelings that may come up during the process. Whatever is important to you, take notes on how you feel when you're on campus.

Many parents feel it's important to write notes down while you're in the moment, while the feelings and impressions are fresh. Most often, your gut will be speaking with you. It's important to follow it, and not overlook red flags that may come up during the recruiting process.

Remember -- it's not always about what coaches are telling you, it's about their actions and how they treat you and how they treat others. You will be seeing the best version of them during the recruiting process, keep track of any uncertainties that may arise and don't overlook those once you're home and sitting down with your family to make a decision!

FULL SCHOLARSHIPS VS. PARTIAL SCHOLARSHIPS

Most NCAA scholarships are not "full rides," and it's important to know because all schools vary with tuition costs, as well as the difference between in-state and out-of-state tuition.

FULL SCHOLARSHIPS: Chances are more likely to receive a full NCAA DI or DII scholarship in "head count" sports — men's and women's basketball, football, women's gymnastics, women's tennis and women's volleyball. Each sport is allowed a maximum number of scholarship athletes, these sports aren't limited on the total amount of aid given.

<u>Example</u>: NCAA DI women's volleyball teams may only carry 12 scholarship athletes, total, as a "head count" sport. The rules do not specify the amount of aid covered among those 12 athletes– all scholarships may be full.

<u>Maximum Scholarship Limits</u>: An institution shall be limited in any academic year to the total number of counters (head count) in each of the following sports:

Football (FBS) - 85
Football (FCS) - 63
Men's Basketball - 13
Women's Basketball - 15
Women's Gymnastics - 12
Women's Tennis - 8
Women's Volleyball - 12

PARTIAL SCHOLARSHIPS: All other sports are considered "equivalency sports," — each sport is allotted a maximum number of total scholarships (varies by sport) that they are able to offer and coaches are able to split up those scholarships among players as they want. Normally, scholarships cover one or multiple expenses including tuition, fees, room and board, books, supplies. For example, wrestling may be allowed to offer 9.9 scholarships per year total, and how that is distributed among the team is decided by the coach. Some athletes may receive tuition, room and board and books while others may just receive financial aid covering part of their tuition.

<u>Example</u>: NCAA Wrestling may only offer a maximum of 9.9 total scholarships, divided up among the roster as each coach decides, as an "equivalency sport."

<u>Maximum Scholarship Limits</u>:

<u>Men's Sports</u>: There shall be a limit on the value (equivalency) of financial aid awards (per that an institution may provide in any academic year to counters in the following men's sports:

Cross Country/Track and Field - 12.6	Soccer - 9.9
Fencing - 4.5	Swimming and Diving - 9.9
Golf - 4.5	Tennis - 4.5
Gymnastics - 6.3	Volleyball - 4.5
Lacrosse - 12.6	Water Polo - 4.5
Rifle - 3.6	Wrestling - 9.9
Skiing - 6.3	

<u>Women's Sports</u>: There shall be a limit on the value (equivalency) of financial aid awards that an institution may provide in any academic year to counters in the following women's sports:

Bowling - 5	Rugby - 12
Cross Country/Track and Field - 18	Skiing - 7
Equestrian - 15	Soccer - 14
Fencing - 5	Softball - 12
Field Hockey - 12	Swimming and Diving - 14
Golf - 6	Triathlon - 5.5 for 2016-17;
Lacrosse - 12	and 6.5 for 2017-18
Rowing - 20	and thereafter.
	Water Polo - 8

THE MONEY TALK: ASKING WHAT YOUR SCHOLARSHIP OFFER WILL COVER

Realistically, for many players, money WILL be a major decision factor when selecting a future school. Colleges vary greatly with the costs of tuition, room and board, course-related books, fees, along with transportation and extra expenses you may have such as cell phone bills, clothing, entertainment. It all adds up—and scholarship money makes a difference for most student-athletes and their families.

There is nothing wrong with being direct and up-front with coaches because at the end of the day, money may be the final factor for most of you. "Am I being considered for a full ride? Am I being considered for a partial scholarship? What would a partial scholarship cover?"

There WILL come a time when you must sit down with your family and decide if it's better for you to go where you can get most or all of your education paid for, or if you have the option of walking-on at your dream school with the help of loans, family support or additional academic/leadership/merit scholarships.

There is a chance you may start out on a partial scholarship and later earn more scholarship aid year-to-year as your contributions to the team increase. On visits, ask other players how the coaching staff handles financial aid at each school.

It's best to have this conversation to help you get a better picture of your options, never feel bad for bringing it up. Coaches are evaluating their options in terms of players, it's your right to evaluate options in terms of financial aid.

There are a lot of options, and a lot to think about...

- Some schools have high tuition costs and if they are only able to offer you a partial scholarship covering books – is that a realistic option for you?

- Would you rather go to a state school on a partial scholarship and graduate with much less debt than going to an expensive out-of-state private school?

- Are you able to secure other loans, pay out-of-pocket, qualify for academic or other scholarships in order to go to your dream school?

- Are you financially able to walk-on at your dream school with the goal of earning an athletic scholarship as a sophomore or junior?

AFTER YOU'VE BEEN OFFERED, HOW LONG DO COACHES HOLD THE SCHOLARSHIP FOR YOU?

With recruiting beginning earlier and earlier, coaches are anxious to get their top prospects committed and finished with the recruiting process. For most players, scholarship offers have an unspoken expiration date!

With each scholarship class coaches determine their needs, position-by-position, and allocate slots based on where they are lacking depth. Once they determine their needs for each signing class, they rate their prospects at each position and work to sell their program to the players who they feel are the best fit.

In many cases, each scholarship slot will have 2-4 equally talented players that the staff would be happy to have... so their attention and efforts will be directed to those key players. As players begin committing to other schools, the priorities of the coaching staff shift to the next-best players available.

There will come a time when coaches may begin to pressure you to commit. If you are a top prospect for them, they may wait your decision out as long as they need to and hold a scholarship for you. If they feel they have other prospects that are equally talented, they may accept one of their commitments and tell you they are no longer recruiting your position.

Some coaches may be honest with you and communicate this possibility to you before it happens, others may not.

Your recruitment to a particular school can end at any time prior to signing your NLI, with little or no warning or explanation. For this reason, if you know in your heart where you'd like to play, it's best to go ahead and commit and focus entirely on your playing season and grades.

Verbal commitments are not binding, NLIs (National Letter of Intent) are. If you are verbally committed to a program but not signed, you have the right to change your mind. But don't just commit to commit and continue looking around, focus instead on making an informed, smart decision.

CAN COACHES PULL SCHOLARSHIP OFFERS AFTER YOU'VE VERBALLY COMMITTED?

Legally, yes. Until you sign an NLI (National Letter of Intent), anything verbal is non-binding on either side. Verbal commitments from players are non-binding as well, and you have the right to change your mind before signing an NLI.

In any sport, there will come a time when coaches will begin pressuring you to commit. Some coaches will be up front with you and say, "We have one scholarship left for your position and you are one of two (or three or four or five) players we'd like to sign for that spot. We'd be happy with either of you, and whoever commits first will get the scholarship." Depending on your talent level—some coaches will wait as long as they need for your decision and others may give you an ultimatum or deadline before moving on to the next-best player on their list. Some may hold a scholarship for you until you make your decision, others will not—it just depends on their interest level.

In some cases, you may not get a warning to make a decision if another player they have equal interest in decides to commit. Your recruitment can end at any time for reasons you can't always control. Experienced coaches can usually be up front with you about how the process is going from their perspective and where you fit in.

WHAT YOU NEED TO KNOW ABOUT COMMITTING

Committing to a coach and program will be one of the most exciting and proud achievements of your life. It can also be a pressure-filled situation, as many coaches will begin to put pressure on you at some point during the recruiting process to get you to commit on their schedule, and not your own.

In the moment, you may feel like you don't want to lose an opportunity -- and realistically, some coaches may tell you there are two (or three, four, five) equally talented players that the coaches are interested in signing but only one scholarship left and ready for the first taker.

The decision is ultimately yours, and use your best judgement based on the number of opportunities that are coming your way. But overall, it's best not to commit to a program unless you are happy and excited about the opportunity. One of the toughest things to do is to go back and decommit a few months down the road or to actually enroll in the school, only to transfer in a year or two.

If a school is genuinely interested in signing you and you're dealing with a quality coach, they will wait as long as they need to for your commitment, and for you to be entirely comfortable in the situation. A great coach who really wants you for their program won't likely pressure you to do something you're not entirely comfortable with.

And lastly, in order to commit to a program you must have a legitimate scholarship offer. I've worked for programs and received calls from prospects who called to commit, who hadn't yet been offered scholarships -- only receiving mail. You have to understand where you are in the process and how serious a coach is about signing you -- just because you are receiving mail or a questionnaire, doesn't necessarily mean that you are in scholarship consideration right now.

MORE TIPS - STAY UPDATED!
Sign up for a online subscription with no monthly commitment at www.1001RecruitTips.com to help guide you through the process!

ACTION STEPS: DEVELOPING & NARROWING YOUR LIST

- YOUR DECISION FACTORS: SIT DOWN AND DECIDE THE 2-3 FACTORS THAT ARE REALLY IMPORTANT TO YOU (SEE EXAMPLES ON PAGE 110). CONTINUE TO GO BACK TO THESE FACTORS AND TRY TO KEEP YOUR DECISION BASED ON YOUR NEEDS! WHETHER IT'S YOUR MAJOR, ACADEMIC PRESTIGE, EARLY PLAYING TIME, DISTANCE FROM HOME, PATH TO THE PROS, CONFERENCE AFFILIATION, PERCENTAGE OF COSTS COVERED, INTERNSHIP OPPORTUNITIES, ETC. WHATEVER IS REALLY IMPORTANT TO YOU IS WHAT YOU NEED TO KEEP IN THE FOREFRONT. COACHES WILL GIVE YOU 100 REASONS TO SELECT THEIR SCHOOL, BUT DON'T GET LOST IN ALL THE FLASH AND CREATIVITY THAT THEY WILL THROW AT YOU. STICK TO YOUR PRIMARY NEEDS AND GOALS WHEN EVALUATING OPPORTUNITIES.

- IMPORTANT FACTORS THAT WILL HELP ME MAKE MY DECISION:
  _____
  _____
  _____

- DEVELOP YOUR QUESTIONS: IT'S NOT JUST UP TO THE COACHES TO DO THEIR RESEARCH AND FIND THE BEST FIT FOR THEM, IT'S ALSO ABOUT YOU FINDING THE BEST FIT. COACHES WANT YOU TO ASK QUESTIONS AND BE INTERESTED IN THE PROCESS, DON'T HOLD BACK.

- MY ACADEMIC QUESTIONS:
  _____
  _____
  _____
  _____
  _____
  _____

- MY ATHLETIC/TEAM QUESTIONS:
  _____
  _____
  _____
  _____
  _____
  _____

NCAA RECRUIT TIPS: 7 STEPS TO A SCHOLARSHIP

- CAMPUS VISITS- UNOFFICIAL & OFFICIAL VISITS: IF POSSIBLE, START GETTING OUT TO DIFFERENT CAMPUSES, EVEN TO SCHOOLS THAT HAVE SHOWN INTEREST IN YOU, THAT YOU MAY NOT BE INTERESTED IN YET. YOU CAN'T JUDGE A SCHOOL BASED ON WHAT YOU THINK YOU KNOW ABOUT THEM, YOU MAY GET THERE AND REALLY LIKE THE ENVIRONMENT. AND VICE VERSA, YOU MAY HAVE YOUR HEART SET ON A SCHOOL, TO ONLY GET THERE AND NOT LIKE THE CAMPUS ENVIRONMENT. CAMPUS VISITS ARE ONE OF THE MOST IMPORTANT ASPECTS OF THE PROCESS! YOU CAN GET THERE AND SEE IT FOR YOUR OWN EYES, AND MORE IMPORTANTLY, GET TO MEET PEOPLE PERSONALLY AND GET A FEEL FOR THE TEAM ENVIRONMENT. WRITE DOWN YOUR NOTES WHILE IN THE MOMENT AND KEEP A NOTEBOOK DETAILING ALL OF YOUR VISITS AND CONVERSATIONS WITH COACHES.

- FULL VS. PARTIAL SCHOLARSHIP OPPORTUNITIES: WITH SCHOOLS THAT ARE SINCERELY INTERESTED IN YOU, AND ARE RECRUITING YOU, THERE WILL COME A TIME WHEN YOU NEED TO FIND OUT IF THEY ARE EVALUATING YOU FOR A FULL OR PARTIAL SCHOLARSHIP, AND WHAT TUITIONS MAY BE AT THOSE UNIVERSITIES. IS THERE A REALISTIC OPPORTUNITY THAT THEY WILL OFFER YOU A SCHOLARSHIP, AND IF SO, WHAT WILL THE SCHOLARSHIP COVER?

- MONEY TALK WITH COACHES AND FAMILY: SIT DOWN WITH YOUR FAMILY AND DISCUSS THE REALISTIC OPPORTUNITIES, AND SITUATIONS YOU MAY HAVE TO CHOOSE FROM. SOME PROGRAMS MAY ONLY BE ABLE TO OFFER YOU A SMALL PARTIAL SCHOLARSHIP BUT HAVE A HIGH TUITION. GET A REALISTIC PICTURE OF HOW MUCH YOUR FAMILY WILL BE ABLE TO CONTRIBUTE TO TUITION, AS WELL AS WHAT TYPE OF LOANS AND OTHER SCHOLARSHIPS YOU MAY BE ABLE TO QUALIFY FOR. FIND OUT IF YOU NEED A FULL RIDE OR IF YOU HAVE SOME FLEXIBILITY WITH OTHER OPTIONS TO HELP PAY FOR SCHOOL WHEN MAKING YOUR SELECTION.

STEP #5
HOW TO HELP YOUR CAUSE

"Setting goals is the first step in turning the invisible into the visible."
– ANTHONY ROBBINS

"Nothing changes if nothing changes."

"When everything seems like an uphill struggle, just think of the view from the top."

NCAA RECRUIT TIPS: 7 STEPS TO A SCHOLARSHIP

COACHES ARE EVALUATING EVERYTHING ABOUT YOU

When making decisions about which players to offer, once coaches have decided that you have the athletic talent to potentially be a prospect for them-- they begin evaluating you entirely. They watch your behavior on the bench, how you take coaching, how you interact with your teammates, how you react when the game or play doesn't go your way, your approach to practice, who you are hanging out with, who you are influenced by. Believe me, they are watching EVERYTHING – not just evaluating your skill, size and speed when it comes to actually offering you a scholarship.

GREAT PLAYERS ARE A DIME A DOZEN!

WHAT MAKES YOU UNIQUE

If you are looking for an edge in recruiting, a way to separate yourself from the other players at your level and to climb into the next level of competition—think about how you can become unique, how can you separate yourself? What can you become a specialist in?

Sure, all coaches are looking for scorers and elite speed and size. But as every player chases the leading scorer title, starting pitcher title, leading rusher title, think about other ways that you can separate yourself, especially by doing the work that few players want to do—the dirty work. The rebounding, the blocking, special teams... the list goes on and on.

Not only do I know college players who earned scholarships this way but I know college players who went on to have long- term professional careers because of this approach! What can make you unique? What can you become a specialist at? Free throws, steals, blocking, punt returns yards after the catch, ball security, breaking the first, second, third tackles consistently. Are you the go-to guy on third- down conversions—not necessarily the deep ball guy but the guy who consistently move the chains on third or fourth down?

Do the dirty work that most other players don't want to do and you will have a better opportunity to be discovered and promoted up the depth chart. Take pride in your specialty!

In basketball, in nearly every interview you can hear coaches complaining about rebounding. Very few coaches are ever content with how they do on the boards, even if they are winning the battle in most games. And, undoubtedly, those basketball teams that are in championship contention... they are head and shoulders better in rebounding than every other team. Coaches are searching to find a player who can get them a major rebounding and defensive edge while most players are

NEVER FEEL POWERLESS. YOU ALWAYS HAVE THE POWER TO WORK HARDER AND PREPARE HARDER, DROP THE NEGATIVE ATTITUDE!

just concerned with their points per game average. THERE is your chance to become a difference-maker, a starter or even a scholarship player!

Every sport provides similar opportunities... think about the skills that you can bring to a team that aren't what every other player is chasing but will help your team win games. THAT will be a way to create buzz and may help you get recruited.

TIMING IS EVERYTHING

Entering your senior year of high school, take a look at the rosters of the schools that you are interested in. What will the roster look like when you are a freshman? Are they loaded at your position or are they starting jobs going to be wide open?

Take into consideration players who are redshirting, players who will most likely leave school early for the draft and players who will be graduating... Where might you fit in on the depth chart? This is exactly how coaches base their needs, what position will we be thin at? They ask themselves, "What is our biggest need?" They'll also ask: "What position has the most depth? Are we even recruiting for that position?"

When you begin to get a chance to talk to coaches at different schools, ask them how many players in your graduating high school class—at your position—do they plan to sign? How many players at your position have already committed? In some cases, they may not plan on signing any players at your position, so you could be wasting your time, especially if it is late in your senior year.

Coaches get daily inquiries from talented recruits—but who play position that they are no longer recruiting for that signing class. If a school has four scholarship QBs who will still be on the roster by the time you get there, then it's not likely they will sign another. If a basketball team is guard-heavy, they will be looking to add bigs in the next class. Do the math! Ask the coaches, especially if you are a senior!

Life is about timing—and if your position isn't needed at the time, it'll be a big waste of your effort if you're chasing a school that has no need for your position. Keep an eye on transfers, players kicked off the team or de-commitments of recruits at your position but also be smart enough to look at other schools that have a NEED for you.

NCAA RECRUIT TIPS: 7 STEPS TO A SCHOLARSHIP

8 TIPS TO HELP YOU GAIN WEIGHT
PLEASE CONSULT YOUR DOCTOR FOR NUTRITION AND DIETING ADVICE

Here are some basic, non-calorie counting tools:

#1 – You must keep a food log! If you don't know your consumption, then how can you add to it? This is a simple numbers game. If you are eating five things a day and not getting the results you want, then go to six things. If you get up to eight items per day eaten and still see no results then it's time to evaluate what you are consuming.

#2 – A few good foods to add that are calorie-dense are bagels, peanut butter, walnuts, almonds, milk, eggs, ice cream, oatmeal and yogurt.

#3 – Stay away from high fat foods that have empty calories!

#4 – Thinking About Supplements? Multi-vitamins, Vitamin D... there is no real substitute for food! Protein, fish, pork, chicken, beef, meat, dairy, nuts.... A serving size is the palm of your hand (at each square).

#5 – NO FRIED FOOD if possible!!!

#6 – Follow the instruction of your coaches.

#7 – If you can't chew it, blend it! Remember, all calories count!! Make smoothies!

#8 – Other quick and healthy food choices are fruit (fresh, canned, dried), low-fat granola bars, whole grain bread/toast, dry cereals (with at least 3 grams of fiber per serving), eggs (may be boiled), pita with hummus, cottage cheese, canned tuna or salmon.

25 TIPS TO BECOME A BETTER LEADER

#1- Don't blame anyone, ever. If times get tough, put the team on your back and say, "I should/could have done more." And understand and believe in that statement – you can always lead everyone to do more. Never throw your teammates or coaches under the bus. Even if they probably deserve it, your reactions will only make the situation worse. If necessarily, pull them aside one-on-one.

#2- Realize that it's up to you. If you are a junior or a senior- you NEED to become a leader. If you are one of the most talented players on the team, you NEED to be a leader. The lockerroom is waiting for someone to SPEAK UP and STEP UP—this starts with you!

#3- During tough times ENCOURAGE those teammates or units that are failing. Urge them to keep fighting!! Support them. Tell them you have their back and know what they are capable of. Offer to join them for extra practice time. Let them know that you believe in them and these tough times will soon pass.

#4- "I may not say much but when I speak, people listen." – If these words come out of your mouth that means you need to SPEAK more often. That means people respect you. That means you have a responsibility.

#5- Invite the team or your position group to your house – extra time together away from the facility helps TREMENDOUSLY. Cook dinner, play video games, watch sports, watch movies, whatever. ANY time that you spend together helps, initiate the effort! Do it on a consistent basis. Set up a weekly tradition.

#6- Leadership is contagious!! Leaders create other leaders. It starts with one—let that be you. Your leadership will cause a ripple effect in your team. If you bring relentless and positive energy to everything that you do they will begin to mirror you.

#7- Eliminate distractions that are holding you back – junk food, video games, academic issues, partying, drama, negative friends. When players see their leaders becoming more serious, they will also begin to sacrifice and make smarter decisions. What you will gain in the future by cutting those distractions will motivate you.

#8- Initiate extra offseason work—bring the energy, set the pace! Have a positive and relentless attitude!! Personal and team improvements happen in the offseason—not during your season! Set the schedule, set the standards, set the positive attitude.

#9- Help your team build trust in each other – no championships are won when a team lacks trust in each other. To be successful, you need teammates that trust each other and a coaching staff who trusts their players. Show your teammates that you trust them. Give your coaches a reason to trust you. Trust begins with simply being where you are supposed to be when you are supposed to be there!

#10- Come 15 minutes early and stay 15 minutes late – Come to the weightroom or film room on off days and bring your unit or teammates to do quality work, put in the same effort as if your coaches are there. Multiply the extra time by the number of teammates who join you—it adds up quickly!

#11- Show that you CARE – You care about the team and you care about WINNING! Once you decide to quit on your team and just put in minimum effort so will everyone else.

#12- Be in the lockerroom as much as you can, create an environment where team wants to be. Music, attitude, conversation—create a positive environment that people want to hang out in.

#13- Academics – call out younger players who are slipping to get it together – raise expectations for them to be responsible!! They will follow your lead. Make it cool to be on the Honor Roll!

#14- Realize and be sensitive that teammates may have outside issues (family, depression, addiction, injury) going on. Be a listener or supporter. Pull troubled teammates aside. Any distractions off-the-field can keep you away from success; do what you can to help your teammates who are going through off-the-field troubles.

#15- Fights are the biggest reason for suspensions and expulsions (and sometimes losses) – When you see teammates scuffling on or off- campus, break it up or diffuse the situation! If one player fights, usually everyone fights. Be the calming voice in heated situations. You want teammates who are committed and focused enough on winning to walk away.

#16- Go by your coach's offices for 10 minutes a few times a week – spend time with the assistant coaches and coordinators. Get to know your coaches. Ask them what you can be doing to get better.

#17- Hold your teammates to high expectations in every area – if you are successful, they'll listen!

#18- You can be more influential than your coaches, realize that your messages are heard—good and bad.

#19- Cut the nonsense at inappropriate times (meetings, practice, film, lift). If your teammates see that you are serious when you need to be, they will focus too.

#20- Help with recruiting talent once on a college campus—host top recruits, be positive. The coaches are working their butts off to bring in the best players and if you want to win, you should be doing so as well.

#21- Eliminate the negativity in the lockerroom. Establish a NO TOLERANCE attitude for complaining and backstabbing among teammates. Negativity never will win championships. Cut it off immediately! Help feuding teammates to get to the root of their problems and to put them behind them.

#22- Get over losses – be positive and move on – brighter days ahead. Get those around you to believe! Frustration makes quitting easier, get your teammates to PUSH PAST that layer of frustration and focus on doing better the next time.

#23- Get the fans involved, you will need them all season! Appreciate them at school, invite them to games, pump up crowd at key times. Win or lose, thank them for coming!

#24- Talk to your coaches if you or a teammate has a major issue that could hurt team (legal, health, academic, eligibility)—the quicker they hear it, the quicker they can address it – it is what is best for the team.

#25- Praise teammates when they do something great. If you are a leader in front of the media, do it publicly. Don't overdo it but make a point to pat teammates on the back for their improvements. People like recognition and once they begin to get it, they will strive for even more. Motivate the backups and practice players, they don't get much acknowledgement for their hard work.

YOU WILL NEVER
EXCUSE
YOUR WAY INTO A CHAMPIONSHIP!

10 SACRIFICES YOU CAN MAKE TO BECOME A BETTER PLAYER

#1 – VIDEO GAMES: Put the controller down!!! Play only on the weekend or give them up all together. Use that time during the week for homework or preparing for the ACT or SAT.

#2 – Go out to the field or court 15 minutes early and stay 15 minutes late to get in extra drills every day. Encourage teammates to join you. Extra practice will help you separate yourself if it's taken seriously on a daily basis.

#3 – Stop eating fried foods, processed foods, candy and fast food. Add more fruit and vegetables to your diet.

#4 – Keep your body pure – No drinking, smoking or drugs!

#5 – Make getting enough sleep a priority. Go to bed early and take naps when possible.

#6 – Wake up an hour early a few times per week to get in extra conditioning. BONUS – Waking up early will help build mental toughness!

#7 – Get position-specific drills in EVERY DAY of the offseason! Ask your coach which drills will help you that you can do on your own. Elite players use the offseason to improve, not just to stay in shape. Select position-specific drills you need improvement on and focus on them every day of the offseason.

#8 – Drink more water! Eliminate sodas and don't overdo it with extra sugar from juice and sport drinks.

#9 – Give up the negative people and influences in your life. Most times, you know exactly WHO and WHAT is holding you back from your dreams and goals. These people and issues are toxic to your future! They are draining you of positive energy which is a NECESSITY on your path to success!

#10 – Get a part-time job (grocery store, mall, restaurant, valet, hospital, construction, moving company) to save up money to attend camps and combines or for travel to visit schools. Do not allow money to be an excuse! A job will also help you build maturity and mental toughness!

14 WAYS TO IMPROVE TIME MANAGEMENT

#1 – Chase greatness and everything else will come – Too many players are too focused on getting all of the media attention and playing the popularity contest that they never develop into great players. They put more focus on those external rewards than becoming great. I've been a part of a BCS (now FBS) National Championship team and worked with Super Bowl Champions and Pro Bowl players, truly great athletes eventually have the world at their feet but they put 99% of their focus on being a beast on the field or court FIRST and know that everything else will come their way. Athletes who chase all of the rewards before they chase championships end up empty-handed!

NCAA RECRUIT TIPS: 7 STEPS TO A SCHOLARSHIP

#2 – The hardest part about being in a relationship while juggling school and sports is dealing with someone who brings DRAMA to your life! RUN AWAY from dating someone who is constantly picking fights or dragging negative chaos into your life, they only get you worked up, spinning in circles and wasting your energy. They genuinely don't respect the fact that you are trying to accomplish things in your life and will only get worse when success comes your way. A non-drama, healthy relationship won't hold you back from anything, be sure put quality effort into the time you spend with your significant other.

#3 – A majority of problems players run into are self-inflicted. Sure, there are problems you can't help (injuries, family situations) but there are too many other factors that you CAN control. Too many players that I've been around have been brought down by drugs, legal issues, their relationship, laziness or a bad attitude. Be real with yourself and eliminate all of the distractions that you can eliminate. It will be challenging enough to overcome setbacks you can't control, why purposely add extra negativity that you CAN control. If you want success, keep successful people in your circle. If you want drama, spend your time with drama! Don't complain or blame the world when these bad habits come back and take your career away. It will happen!

#4 – Be where you are – If you are with your girlfriend, boyfriend or parents, don't be texting, taking calls or playing video games. Spend quality time with them. If you are working on a paper, don't spend 2 hours arguing with your girlfriend or boyfriend because a paper that can take you one hour to write will take you four or five hours or end up incomplete. Your friends and family will appreciate 100% of your attention in shorter periods of time than if you are constantly distracted or interrupted.

#5 – Just do what is asked of you the first time. I watch players go in circles all day, trying to get out of extra punishments and trouble they've gotten themselves into, problems they could have avoided by just doing what was asked of them in the first place. Go to class. Go to study hall. Be at practice on time. Be everywhere 5 minutes early and you won't have to worry about detention, punishment workouts or suspensions. If you just do what is asked of you by your teachers and coaches, you will be fine. If you skip class, skip a workout, sleep in class, you will have to face the punishment and that will likely add an extra hour or two to your day.

#6 – TV/Internet– You get sucked in and will go from checking your Facebook 'real quick' to spending 2 hours browsing. Pretend that you are on a diet, you can only have a bite of that cake but you can't eat the whole thing. Don't get sucked into the couch, computer or TV for more than 15 or 20 minutes if you have a big to-do list.

#7 – Quit talking about how much you have to do and how you'll never possibly get it done and just do it. People yap on and on about how they have too much to do and if they would just shut the door and work on a few things, they will feel a lot less pressure. Put your phone on silent, don't log on the internet, shut your door, go to the library, find a hiding place where you can get your work done and it will eliminate some of the pressure you are feeling.

#8 – Get up an hour early – If you need extra studying or conditioning, get up at 6am and do it. You are much less likely to get distracted by others and as a bonus – it builds mental toughness. If you are can become disciplined enough to get up an extra hour or two earlier you are IMPROVING and building MENTAL TOUGHNESS!

#9 – Are you doing too much? Are you involved in too many sports, clubs, family issues, friend issues? You have to really focus on the two or three things that are really important to you and may have to give up some of the extra distractions that aren't helping you get to where you want to go. For a week, keep track of how much you spend your time on hour-by-hour, you might be surprised.

#10 – Set a study schedule – When I was in college I tried to get to the library Monday-Thursday until 10pm, even if I had no homework due the next day. At times, the library became the hangout spot so I found a different quiet spot on campus to do my work and reading at. There is always work that you can do to get ahead. If you put in the consistent work on those days, you can enjoy the weekend. In college it is near impossible to get any work done in the dorms, go somewhere else and you'll drastically cut the hours you need to finish assignments and prepare, freeing up more time for YOU!

#11 – Prioritize what is important to you. When I was part of a BCS National Championship team – our coach did little outside of developing our players, self-scouting, breaking down opponents, gameplanning, recruiting and creating events or programs that would improve our team. He had his family around the facility often and his wife and kids joined us for dinner after practice sometimes. He rarely got dragged away for fundraising, marketing or other activities unless it meant a big addition to our program. School, sports, family, relationships... Write down your list of a few priorities and focus on the top things that you must have. Everything else, slowly eliminate. If it doesn't help you improve in those areas, drop it.

#12 – Put down the video game controller – Save it for the weekend or offseason. Hours, days, weekends are wasted this way!

#13 – Get sleep when you can – Sneak in naps during the day and try to go to bed early. Sleep will help you make fewer mistakes at practice and in games and puts you in a better mood. When you are tired you are cranky and get frustrated and forgetful. It's hard to do everything that is asked and expected of you if you are exhausted. Sneak in naps whenever you can.

#14 – Successful college and pro coaches are some of the most efficient people on the planet. They don't waste a minute. They go from a player meeting to recruit call to film session to scheduling games for next season to planning their travel schedule to checking on their child to a budget meeting with the Athletic Director to a radio phone interview to practice without daydreaming for a minute. It takes that kind of efficiency and focus to become successful on a high level. Are there things you can eliminate from your daily schedule that can cut 10 minutes, 30 minutes or an hour? It all adds up very quickly!

WHEN YOU ACT LIKE YOU DON'T CARE YOU ARE JUST PUTTING UP A WALL BECAUSE YOU DON'T ACTUALLY BELIEVE IN YOURSELF. WINNERS SHOW THAT THEY CARE – WIN OR LOSE!

NCAA RECRUIT TIPS: 7 STEPS TO A SCHOLARSHIP

DIRECT LINE OF COMMUNICATION

Contact the schools that are interested in recruiting you or that you have an interest in and give them your contact info and ask to have a questionnaire sent to you. If you are in contact with any coaches, give them your home address, home phone number, cell phone number and email address so they can send you information and call you directly.

Some high school coaches hide mail from their players and don't always pass along phone messages that coaches leave. If you are a great player, there may be other schools out there that are interested in recruiting you that you may never hear about. If certain coaches have tried to make contact with you or anyone in your circle, call the school and give them your direct info!

Each year I reached out to several coaches to get direct contact information for their players and would get about 25% of them telling me that we need to go through them directly to speak with the player. There's always another group of coaches who don't respond at all. With technology, our coaches could reach out to them on Facebook and get their contact info directly. Players whose coaches kept us from them were happy to hear from us when we went around their high school coaches! In many cases, when the coach finally gets in touch with the player, they had no idea we were interested. Not every prep coach is looking out for your best interested and sharing all of the information with you.

Nobody should be blocking this knowledge from you so it's best if the college coaches know how to contact you directly to avoid this issue.

RESPOND TO QUESTIONNAIRES

At every program I've worked we've gotten daily calls, letters and emails requesting a questionnaire. This isn't usually a helpful or efficient way to get on a coach's radar, particularly at many Division I schools. Again, the only true way to get the school to recruit you is if they see you play in person or on video.

The exception is if a school SENDS you a questionnaire, a questionnaire that you didn't call and request yourself. You should definitely fill it out and return it, it means they have gotten your name from a trusted source and want to do some more research on you and may contact you at some point.

On the flip side, when you call and request a questionnaire, it may not get looked at or added to the database when you return it. When people request questionnaires they are often coded before they go out and are not always evaluated when they are returned, particularly at more competitive schools. Cut to the chase and send your film!

SOCIAL MEDIA & RECRUITING: 16 TIPS BEFORE YOU POST

BE SMART! You may be trying to impress your friends, but you may be turning off the coaches who have the power to offer you a scholarship. Is broadcasting certain thoughts and opinions REALLY that important if it could cost you a scholarship opportunity?

Think, the head coach at your dream school could be out there saying this... "I'm ready to offer you a scholarship and I can't find your cell phone number so I go to hit you up on Twitter... then I read your tweets." What will their next move be? Believe me, they're reading them!!

#1- It's not just what you say, but who you are connected to! When you comment on other people's pictures or profiles, or like graphic or vulgar pictures, there is a good chance it's showing up in coaches' feeds!

As a prospective college athlete understand that not only are you being evaluated by your skills, size, speed and grades, your character is also under the microscope. In life you are warned to surround yourself with good people. Online, the people you follow, interact with and comment on will show up. Choose those people you follow and interact with wisely!

#2- In a society where players from Top 25 programs and many Division I teams make negative headlines on ESPN for their tweets and status updates (within hours or minutes after posts) – yes, many coaches eliminate prospects who show poor character, judgment and language in social media. These poor-taste posts won't just have your name on it, they will have the university's name attached to it too! Coaches know that how you carry yourself in high school will likely carry over to the college level and only become magnified. If you are Top 25 talent, you will be under a MAJOR magnifying glass even before you commit to a school!

#3- Understand that if you can't handle the power of social media as a high school player, a coach will have serious doubt that you can handle it as a college player on a much bigger stage.

#4- Since coaches are trying to get to know you better, almost all of them search social media accounts for clues. Just like the film doesn't lie, neither does the negativity you post on social media!

#5- Just because you didn't write it, a RT still shows up in your timeline and is just as bad!

#6- Keep your tweets and updates free of bad language and never retweet vulgar tweets. Never tweet or RT about illegal activities such as drugs, underage drinking, bullying, fighting, stealing, etc.

#7- Social media can be used for good, share links of your highlights with coaches via Facebook or Twitter! It may not help, but it just may be the way you can get your video in front of the right coaches, especially if you can't find their direct email!

> **EVERY COLLEGE COACH THAT I KNOW SAY THEY'VE STOPPED RECRUITING A PLAYER BASED ON THEIR ONLINE STATUS UPDATES BECAUSE OF DISRESPECTFUL LANGUAGE.**

#8- Even if it's a song lyric, not many college coaches are young enough to know that and read it as your opinion or thought!

#9- Stop with the subtweeting, it's not a good look!

#10 – On the flip side, always tweeting about getting a workout in or extra cardio or position drills isn't always convincing. If you spend so much time posting on social media about how hard you're working out, a lot of coaches might be skeptical about exactly how much time you're putting in to get better.

#11- Coaches are not able to communicate with prospects until a certain date, each sport varies. Social media rules are based on the dates that apply to 'general correspondence,' such as an email. When NCAA coaches are allowed to send 'general correspondence,' they are allowed to follow or friend a prospects' social media account. After this date, they are also allowed to send private messages on Facebook or DMs on Twitter. (See page 88 for more info).

#12- You need to keep your social media PG, even if it is protected. A screenshot can get out quick and be used against you!

#13- Coaches are NOT allowed to publicly comment on a prospect's page or like their pictures or statuses—at any time! They can't @mention or @reply to prospects on Twitter.

#14- If there is a change in coaching staff, it's not necessary for you to tweet your emotional opinions. Take a breath, sit on it for a couple days and let everything play out before blasting out some comments you will regret in a week or two. Just because people ask you for your opinion, that doesn't mean you have to give it. Use good judgement!

#15- Nobody says you HAVE to have social media accounts, or have to post on social media accounts. You can have accounts and not post status updates or pictures, or you can deactivate accounts all together and focus more time and attention on chasing that scholarship!

#16- When in doubt about posting something, ask yourself: "Who is it more important to impress—college coaches or high school classmates?" Also ask yourself, "Am I comfortable saying this in front of my mom, grandma, little sister, teacher, principal, high school coach or college coaches recruiting me?"

IF YOU WANT MORE SUCCESS, SURROUND YOURSELF WITH THOSE THAT HAVE SUCCESS. IF YOU WANT DRAMA, SURROUND YOURSELF WITH DRAMA!

DON'T BECOME A PEST

Calling or emailing a program every day is a quick way to get noticed, but not in a good way. Your biggest allies in the process can be the staff that answer the phone and generic emails, so it would be in your best interest to not become a pest. They quickly recognize you and soon stop passing your daily messages along.

Programs get daily calls from players and their families telling them that they are the one and only school that they want to play for.

While it's a nice gesture, that means nothing to those coaches if they aren't interested in your talent. For this reason, one of the most important factors that I will stress to you is that a coach can't evaluate your talent and offer you a scholarship (or a walk-on spot) without seeing you play in person or on video first. What does that mean to you? It means that blowing up the phone lines will not help you. Get your highlight video ready BEFORE calling or emailing coaches at schools that you are interested in and save yourself some trouble.

One of the best pieces of advice I heard about preparing for a job interview was that you need to convince the hiring manager that THEY need YOU—not that they need to hire you because you really need or want the job, employers could care less about YOUR needs and wants during the interview process. Employers want the best and most talented person for the job. Same with coaches. Coaches need to NEED a player with your skills to be interested in recruiting you. Just because it's your dream to play for a certain school, it doesn't mean that they will have any added interest in recruiting you if you don't have the talent to compete there and be successful for their program.

> **WE ALL HAVE THE SAME FEARS AND INSECURITIES-- OUR RESULTS DEPEND ON HOW WE RESPOND TO THOSE DOUBTS WE PLACE ON OURSELVES.**

So, once you get your video ready to mail or email your #1 goal will be trying to get SOMEONE there to confirm that it's been received and to get SOMEONE to watch it. You need to follow-up with them a day or two after it arrives and confirm the name of who will be watching it. If you aren't getting any feedback, you need to call back and see if you can get in contact with a grad assistant or Director of Operations and see if they are able to watch it. This should take you no more than three phone calls!

Too often, players will call multiple times per day... FOR DAYS. This is a big DON'T—you will become "that kid." Same goes for parents and coaches—it's unnecessary to call 5 times in a week. It won't help your cause!

NCAA RECRUIT TIPS: 7 STEPS TO A SCHOLARSHIP

If you aren't getting any answers from the recruiting coach or grad assistant, back off and call back in a few weeks. If you are not a senior, back off and call early in the off-season once the coaches may have more time.

As discussed earlier, it never hurts to have one of your prep coaches call. It's good manners for college coaches to call back prep coaches, so use this gesture to your advantage. If you didn't have any luck getting someone to evaluate your video, ask your current coaches if they will call on your behalf. Remember—a coach probably won't (and shouldn't) call schools for you that are way outside of your talent level. Be realistic when asking for favors— but if your coach agrees to call for you, it would never hurt your chances!

ACTION STEPS: HOW TO HELP YOUR CAUSE

- **BECOME A SPECIALIST:** WHICH 1-2 FUNDAMENTAL SKILLS CAN YOU FOCUS ON THAT MAY BE ABLE TO HELP YOU GET AN EDGE IN RECRUITING AT YOUR POSITION?

WHAT SKILLS I CAN SPECIALIZE IN TO HELP MY TEAM & RECRUITING:
_____
_____
_____

- **IMPROVE YOUR STRENGTHS:** WHAT ARE THE TOP FEW SKILLS THAT YOU ARE SOLID AT, EVEN THE MOST BASIC ONES? HOW CAN YOU CONTINUE TO IMPROVE IN THOSE AREAS?

WHAT STRENGTHS CAN I IMPROVE ON TO HELP MY TEAM & RECRUITING:
_____
_____
_____

- **IMPROVE AS A LEADER:** IN JUST A FEW WAYS, HOW CAN YOU BEGIN TO STEP UP AS A LEADER FOR YOUR POSITION GROUP, CLASS OR TEAM? COME UP WITH 1-2 REGULAR HABITS YOU CAN START THAT WILL HELP INFLUENCE YOUR TEAMMATES IN A POSITIVE WAY. SEE PAGE 132 FOR EXAMPLES.
_____
_____
_____

- **MAKE IMPACTFUL SACRIFICES:** WHAT FEW IMPORTANT SACRIFICES CAN YOU BEGIN TO MAKE THAT WILL HELP YOU IMPROVE ACADEMICALLY AND ATHLETICALLY? SEE PAGE 135 FOR MORE EXAMPLES.

  _____
  _____
  _____

- **MASTER TIME MANAGEMENT:** WHAT TIME-WASTERS CAN YOU ELIMINATE THAT CAN FREE UP MORE TIME FOR YOU TO PREPARE, MORE TIME FOR YOU TO STUDY, MORE TIME FOR YOU TO REST? WHAT CAN YOU CUT OUT FROM YOUR DAY OR WEEK THAT IS UNNECESSARY? SEE PAGE 135 FOR EXAMPLES.

  _____
  _____
  _____

- **BE PROACTIVE:** FOR MOST OF YOU, SCHOLARSHIP OFFERS WON'T JUST COME AND FIND YOU. ALWAYS REMEMBER THAT YOU JUST NEED TO FIND THAT ONE COACHING STAFF WHO BELIEVES IN YOU – AND IT MAY TAKE HUNDREDS OF PHONE CALLS, EMAILS, TWEETS AND LETTERS SENT TO GET THERE! BE PROACTIVE WITH THE PROCESS, YOU CAN'T AFFORD TO JUST SIT BACK AND WAIT FOR COACHES TO COME FIND YOU!

- **GIVE COACHES YOUR DIRECT CONTACT INFO:** TO ELIMINATE ANY CONFUSION OR ISSUES, IT'S BEST TO GIVE YOUR RECRUITING COACHES YOUR DIRECT CONTACT INFO (OR THE PARENT OR MENTOR YOU WANT TO HELP WITH THE PROCESS) SO THAT ALL COMMUNICATION IS GETTING TO THE RIGHT PEOPLE. MOST COLLEGE COACHES ARE ASKING YOUR PREP COACHES AND PARENTS ABOUT HOW TO APPROACH RECRUITING, BE DIRECT AND UP FRONT WITH COACHES ABOUT HOW AND WHERE YOU WOULD LIKE COMMUNICATION TO GO!

- **RESPOND TO QUESTIONNAIRES:** IF A COACH SENT YOU A QUESTIONNAIRE, IT'S AN EARLY SIGN OF INTEREST. RESPOND! AND RESPOND IN A TIMELY MANNER!

STEP #6
IF 'PLAN A' ISN'T WORKING OUT...

"My success wasn't so much due to my intelligence, but the fact that I stuck with problems longer."
– ALBERT EINSTEIN

"When you get to the end of your rope, tie a knot and hang on."
– FRANKLIN D. ROOSEVELT

"Failure defeats losers, failure inspires winners."
– ROBERT KIYOSAKI

"You cannot change your destination overnight, but you can change your direction overnight."
– JIM ROHN

WHEN YOU DON'T FEEL LIKE YOU'RE IMPROVING ATHLETICALLY

Relax—GREATNESS takes time! Players don't develop over weeks or a few months, it takes a year or years to begin to see significant differences. It's up to you to decide if you are willing to put in the time and it's up to you to remain mentally tough. It's not easy, and you're going to have to work your butt off!

It's important to work smart:

#1- You need to set one or two goals—don't overwhelm yourself with many improvements you need to make—just worry about the a few really important ones! Pick one weakness and one strength—what can you become the best at in your school/city/state, and what is your biggest weakness that needs major improvement? Start with just those.

#2- Now, after you have set those goals, put a number on them, make them specific. Make them measurable goals. You may have to pick a position-specific goal and chart your workouts—partner with a teammate and keep track of balls caught/dropped, shots made, batting average, reps in the weight room.

#3- Now give yourself a deadline... many experts say you should work in short-term goals. Six weeks, three months. Don't put a deadline on your goal for a year from now, break it down into smaller, more achievable deadlines.

#4 – Ask your coach for drills. Ask for advice, ask players who are good at you want to be good at, ask them for advice. Often, there are little tips, tricks or minor adjustments you can make that will help you become more efficient and make a big difference.

#5- Write down your goals and put them in a place you will see them every day. Verbalize them. Tell your friends and family your goals—it will make you more likely to stick to them if you are sharing your goals with other people.

#6- Visualize what it would be like to achieve your goals. Close your eyes and spend 10 minutes in silence thinking about what it'll feel like when you hit your goal, what it will feel like when you get that phone call from a coach offering you a scholarship, what it will feel like to be packing for college. Some of the greatest competitors visualize themselves achieving their goals, years before they actually happen. Build that passion within you, it will help you tune out the negativity of your doubters. Visualize, over and over—and then get up and work like heck to make them happen!

Yes, the work you put in today is helping you get there. All those extra workouts add up over an extended period of time—months and months. While you are in high school, your body is still developing and you still may have time to grow a few inches taller and put on some more weight. Keep working—you may not see the results tomorrow or next month but they will make you a better player and give you better chances of playing at the collegiate level!

We may not get there today, we may not get there next week—but we WILL get there if we keep putting in the work!!! I see miracles happen every year, and players make major turn-arounds all the time! Just takes a little extra patience!

COMMITMENT IS A TWO-WAY STREET! YOU WANT YOUR COACHES TO TRUST AND COMMIT TO YOU, YOU MUST TRUST AND COMMIT TO THE THINGS THEY ASK OF YOU.

HOW TO IMPROVE MENTAL TOUGHNESS

Even the best athletes doubt themselves at some point. You will likely have many people tell you that you won't make it, you aren't good enough, that you aren't talented... believe me, it's extremely tough to tune out and ignore, but you must ignore it! What I have learned is this... the people who tell you that you will never make it are often the ones who are most afraid that you will.

To build mental toughness you must commit yourself to becoming the most prepared player on the court/field. When you are prepared, you develop confidence. When you aren't afraid to make mistakes, you develop confidence. When you prepare on a high level, you develop toughness. You expect more of yourself than anyone else. You can withstand the trials. You have prepared hard and are committed to being the last one standing.

The ultimate source of confidence is knowing you are 100% prepared.

AS YOU DEVELOP PHYSICALLY INTO A GREAT PLAYER, YOU MUST DEVELOP MENTALLY AS WELL. YOU MUST TRAIN YOURSELF TO TUNE OUT CRITICISM AND TO WORK THROUGH THE SLUMPS.

Failing isn't scary, even the best athletes fail at some point in their careers. The real failure is not being prepared, failing is not putting yourself in the best position as possible. Failing means you were unprepared. If you try your hardest, work the hardest, that's all you can do. There is no failure in giving it everything you've got.

HOW DO YOU REPAIR CHARACTER ISSUES?

As much as college coaches are researching you as a player and evaluating you physically, they are evaluating you just as much as a person and student. Trust me, most of them do a lot of homework outside of just your height, weight, speed and stats. They want to see the whole picture and understand what type of person you are.

Experienced coaches reach out to several sources in the area when they are interested in a player. The prep coaches, the parents, rival school coaches, AAU coaches, Principals, Guidance Counselors... they don't just ask one person their opinion, they're asking for recommendations from all types of people that players come across. You may be a certain way with your coach, but carry yourself differently in other areas. They want to see an accurate picture of who you are.

Be short and to the point, and tell the coaches that you may have been immature in the past or not handled a situation in the best way that you could, but you learned. If you carry yourself in a mature way in your dealings with them, they can judge for themselves. Walk a straight line, handle your responsibilities– do what you are supposed to do — and your reputation can improve.

If you know these rumors are being said about you, it's okay to address them. If a college coach is legitimately interested in you, be upfront with them. The worst thing you can do at this point is lie about your past. A lot of players have faced adversities, may have acted out immaturely at times, had family problems going on or issues with other players. To be honest, college coaches want to see growth, and maturity, and see that you've moved on from tough situations of your past. If you do have a past, it's okay to be up front with the coaches and prove to them that you have grown up and changed.

College coaches won't want to spend endless time re-hashing injustices you feel you may have faced with playing time, starting jobs, favoritism and politics– it's probably not in your best interest to replay your whole life story to them because in the end, it just makes you look dramatic. Coaches aren't going to want to bring that type of drama to their college campuses and lockerrooms, where these problems will just be magnified. They just don't have the time for it!

If you are looking for a fresh start, put everything in the past. Carry yourself as a college-bound, mature player who is just looking for their opportunity, and who is willing to work hard to get there!

NOT HEARING ANYTHING BACK FROM COACHES AFTER SENDING VIDEO

First off, this is normal for many players. You may have hundreds of unreturned phone calls and emails—I'm not exaggerating! It's not always easy. For most of you, it won't be easy.

There could be a few issues:

#1- Are you old enough for coaches to contact you? The NCAA limits DI and DII schools, dates when coaches are allowed to contact you vary by sport—see page 88. They may not be responding because they are not allowed to.

#2- Are you sending your film to a specific person? The coach who recruits your area? NEVER send your film to a generic email address like basketball@school.edu. Nobody may be checking it.

#3- Have you followed up with the recruiting coach who you sent it to? Coaches get hundreds of unsolicited emails from recruits each month. Sometimes they get lost in the shuffle and are unopened. Coaches have endless responsibilities and don't always have time to watch all unsolicited film (not requested by coaching staff). Follow up to help your chances!

#4- Have you limited yourself? If you aren't being recruited and are a junior or senior, send your film and Student-Athlete Resume to schools within 250-400 mile radius. They may not be your dream schools or where you want to sign, but it's easier to gain interest and get in contact with coaches if you have other offers, no matter what level of play. Positive momentum can help you, both mentally and in getting a few minutes of time from other coaches.

If your film isn't working, you need to try a few other paths. There are "8 Reasons Why Athletes are Recruited (see page 34)." You may need to try a different angle.

If you still aren't gaining interest you may need to consider going to a Junior College for a year or two or to try to make a team as a Walk-On. You may need to consider academic or other types of scholarship opportunities and pursue walk-on opportunities.

I'VE STARTED SEVERAL GAMES AND JUST GOT BENCHED FOR NO REASON. SHOULD I TRANSFER?

Not necessarily – you may think there is "no reason," but your coach may have a valid reason.

From a recruiting standpoint – benching and playing time can effect your recruitment in a few ways:

• Does your benching have anything to do with attitude, grades or work ethic? Is there a "lesson" in the benching that your coach is trying to teach you? Can you talk to your coach about it, and ask what steps you need to take to get back on the field?

• Are you still getting playing time but not starting? Starting plays no role in how you can impact a game, if you are still getting playing time there are ways you can showcase your talent and abilities. Can you still find a way to help your team win and be strong fundamentally at your position, so these abilities can show up on film?

• If another player has passed you on the depth chart, and may be holding on to the top spot, is there another position you can switch to in order to get more playing time? Where can you help your team win?

• There are 8 Reasons Why Players Get Noticed & Recruited (page 34) – getting benched during the season doesn't have to end your chances of earning a scholarship. Can you get noticed in any of the other ways during your time on the bench?

Adversity is going to happen — at the high school level, college level and in real life when you have to get a job. Life is not fair, and often lessons and work ethics taught in sports, can help you get through these adversities in real life.

Even some of the most talented players have had adversities they've had to work through — playing time, injuries, suspensions. College coaches will ask you about the situation if you are being recruited, and they'll also ask your prep coaches and possibly other coaches in the area. College coaches are always trying to get the full picture of what's going on– so they'll ask a lot of sources.

If you are being treated unfairly, someone along the line will usually speak up and voice that. Politics takes place in a lot of organizations, and high school sports are no exception. How you handle the situation will tell coaches a lot about you. Instead of running away or quitting—are there some constructive solutions to the situation?

While it can be a stressful situation for you, use that frustration as fuel. As hard as it is, keep your attitude positive and relentless. Work harder. Practice more. Focus your energy, eliminate distractions. Be better in the classroom and with the playbook. Do everything that is asked of you. Use this situation as motivation, because you will have situations like this happen throughout life and the younger you learn to work through adversity (instead of run from it), will only help you. Be such a great teammate and improved player that you can't be ignored.

While it's hard to remember now, understand that rosters are very fluid. Players move up and down throughout their season and career. Just when you think there will never be another opportunity for you, a door may open. Just work even harder and be ready for your chance when that door opens!

WILL SUSPENSIONS END MY RECRUITMENT?
One of a coach's toughest jobs during the recruiting process is to evaluate the risk vs. reward with players.

All coaches in America ask themselves: "Will I sign a more talented player with off-the-field issues or mistakes in their past... or will I sign a less talented player who has no off-the-field issues?"

Every situation is different and every coaching staff is different – ultimately it's up to the head coach if they want to take a chance on a player with legal or attitude issues. I've worked with some coaches who will take anyone, other coaches who want nothing to do with a player with a past and then some in-between.

Head coaches evaluate these situations on a case-by-case basis. Was it an isolated issue? Did you have family issues going on? Have you gotten away from bad influences? Have you learned, changed, matured? Can you be trusted? Many coaches don't want to bring in a bad apple to their lockerroom if they trust their team, they don't want to disrupt the chemistry in the lockerroom.

In many, not all cases, a player's past is a prediction of the issues they will bring with them to college. If you have a particular attitude or issues within your circle, you will likely bring those issues and negative influences with you to college. Some coaches think you'll never change and other coaches will give you the opportunity to grow up.

If you are talented enough athletically, coaches will look into your issues/mistakes and evaluate. In some cases, they must get approval from the Athletic Director of University President if there is a legal record. Coaches don't just want your side of the story, they will ask as many people with direct knowledge as possible to get a clearer view of the situation and you as a person.

To many coaches, they would rather take a player with no off-field issues because at the end of the day, winning is based on trust. If your coaches can't trust you, you won't win together. And if you are a great athletic talent who keeps finding yourself in trouble, coaches know that if they begin to let you get away with more than the other players on the team, and that is the beginning of the end for a head coach. When players aren't accountable, it's only a matter of time before the coaches are fired.

Your attitude is one of the few things you'll ever be able to control!

WHAT IF THERE IS A CHANGE IN COACHES?

One of the toughest hurdles a player will go through during their career is dealing with a coaching change, especially at the collegiate level. Whether a coach retires, leaves for another school, decides to go coach a pro team or gets fired—emotions run high and the media and critics will pile on the negativity.

What's important to know as a recruit is that when you sign a NLI (National Letter of Intent), you are signing with the university, not the coach. If the coach leaves, you are still bound by the NLI that was signed.

With traditional and social media being so instantaneous, one of the toughest aspects of a coaching change is the fact that players nowadays rarely hear about the change directly from the coach themselves. When players hear it from ESPN, Twitter or friends texting them, they're naturally caught off guard and usually feel disrespected or shocked. Off the bat, they have a tendency to act out emotionally: lash out in the media, skip team meetings and workouts, stop going to class or threaten to go pro. This is normal and natural, people are trying to make decisions based on EMOTIONS.

> **IF YOU DON'T WANT TO BE TRIPLE-CHECKED ON, JUST DO THE THINGS THAT YOU ARE EXPECTED TO DO THE VERY 1ST TIME YOU ARE ASKED. NOTHING MORE, NOTHING LESS.**

It's important to understand that the high rate of turnover in the coaching profession is the prime reason why it's so important for players to feel comfortable at the SCHOOL and in the TOWN without the coach that recruited them there because there is a good chance that the coach may not be there for their entire career.

It's hard for 18-21 year-olds to fully understand but when a coach decides to leave a program, the decision has nothing to do with the players. Coaches take and leave jobs for the pure reasons of #1- the betterment of their family (more money, closer to family and home, a promotion) or #2- a better opportunity to win (bigger budget, bigger fanbase, easier path to a championship). Those are the only two reasons; it is never personal with the players.

It's natural and okay for you to be hurt and frustrated, understand that it is okay for you to take time away from the media, social media and speaking publicly on the matter until you have had enough time for it to sink in and for the university to hire a new coach, you will have time to evaluate the new hire and decide if you would like to keep firm on the commitment or re-open your recruitment.

Early in my career, a coaching change would have been shocking. One of the biggest things that could happen! After my 16 years in athletics, I now understand that it's just part of the business and nearly every team will lose at least one coach every year. It's just the way of life for coaches. Having worked for so many, it'd be safe to say that over 75% are looking for other jobs or being contacted for new positions each off-season, it's just the way it is.

While fans and administration put a lot of their focus (and rightfully so) on the players, there's a whole backbone of the program going through turmoil when there is a transition in head coaches—the assistant coaches, strength coaches, trainers, video coordinators and team operations staff. A head coach is basically responsible for the livelihood of 6-15 full-time staff members and each of their spouses and children. No matter the reason they are gone, nearly everyone else is left hanging and worrying about their job and family. In most cases, everyone lands on their feet but it's a rough few weeks or months until everyone is able to secure a new job.

The outgoing coach may bring some staff with them and it's understood that the incoming coach has 100% freedom to clean house from top to bottom and bring in their own network of trusted staff. Everyone is on their own during this time, these stretches can bring out the worst side of people and have a tendency to be really, really awkward.

STOP LETTING THE LITTLE NEGATIVE THINGS KEEP YOU FROM THE BIG, POSITIVE STEPS YOU NEED TO TAKE.

Give yourself time to decide if you are still excited about your opportunities and the direction of the program, it's perfectly normal for you to keep quiet on the matter and have 'no comment' to media and friends, especially if you are a major Division I prospect. Evaluate the opportunities, community and entire situation before making comments you may regret in a week or two! Understand that in the end you will all be fine, just give the situation time to run its course!

15 TIPS FOR ADJUSTING TO A NEW COACH

#1- Drama doesn't carry over to the new staff, don't waste your time explaining hardships, injustices, favoritisms. The new coaches don't care or have time to hear it! Instead, ask for expectations, goals, suggestions. Finding out what they expect for you is more important than explaining why you have failed in the past! Start fresh, it's time to grow up!

#2- A new coach, whether you agree with the change or not, will bring new attention to your program. There will be fresh blood, increased media attention, new donors, bigger budget, new equipment and new technology. Your program may get a slight or major upgrade when a new coach comes in

#3- When a new coach is hired, this is the time to flush negativity out of the program and start fresh. You will likely have a blank slate (even if you have a negative track record)—this is your chance to "start over" and grow up!

#4- New coaches are going to have you under a microscope and enforcing one thing early: attention to detail. Go to class. Be on time. Do what you're supposed to do when you are supposed to do it.

#5- You will be making your biggest impressions without saying a word, coaches are watching every move their players make. What you DO will tell your coaches more about you than anything you can ever tell them about yourself.

#6- There will be a new way of doing things, Day 1. Learn EXACTLY what your coaches want from you. Do it "their way," not the way you think works best. They will have a new plan they will be implementing immediately. The more you resist early, the tougher (and less successful) the transition will be.

#7- The first impression coaches will get about you are reports on how you handled the coaching transition while there was no head coach in place. Did you skip workouts, skip class, gain 10 pounds? Were you a leader? Did you keep the team together or did you go buck wild?

#8- When players hear the news of a coaching change on Twitter or ESPN, they are naturally caught off guard and feel disrespected but this is the new standard in our world of social media. It's best to not overreact on social media! It's natural to be hurt, so it's best to take some time to yourself, there is no rule that says you MUST comment publicly. When a new coach is hired, take your time and keep all comments positive. If you don't have anything nice to say, don't say anything at all.

#9- When coaches leave a job, it's never personal with the players, don't feel like it's your fault or that you could have done something different. Coaches take new jobs for betterment of their family (more money, closer to home or family) or for the betterment of their career (promotion, easier path to championship, bigger budget). Since there is such a high rate of turnover in coaching, it's critical you pick a school based on other factors besides the head coach.

#10- The new coach has the right to bring in their own assistant coaches. Sometimes they will retain a coach or two from the old staff, but understand it's normal for them to clean house and hire coaches that know their system or who they have relationships with. Once everything settles, your old coaches will be fine and likely land on their feet in a new job within a couple months.

#11- Your new coach will likely run some of your teammates off: players with negative attitudes, poor work ethics often quit or threaten to transfer. It doesn't mean they are a bad coach, it means they were probably poor teammates. (Others may quit because they don't fit the new style of play.) This is normal.

#12- It's natural to keep in contact with your old coach, they were likely a mentor that you had a close relationship with. Keep the conversations free of negative talk but know that it's ok to check in with them or congratulate them on their success in the future.

#13- The depth chart is likely wide open. Use the summer and offseason to work your way up the depth chart. Skill, size and speed are the key factors they are evaluating, BUY IN and get to know their system and style of play backwards and forwards.

#14- Be the first player in, last one to leave—your new coaches will take notice!

#15- Relationships, trust and chemistry take time. You probably feel like that the coaches don't know you or fully trust you yet... and you may feel the same way about them. Invest in getting to know the new staff, it's a two-way street. You feel like they don't know you, well put time in getting to know them!

THE RIGHT TO CHANGE YOUR MIND
Another factor I want to stress to you is that you ALWAYS have the right to change your mind before you sign that National Letter of Intent (NLI). No matter how close to Signing Day, if your heart and gut are raising the red flags on your decision—by all means, follow them! Truthfully, college coaches deal with recruits changing their mind ever year, they will get over it. Most coaches want you to make a decision that is best for you, they understand that if you make a decision that you are not comfortable with in the end, you will likely transfer in a year or two, and that effects everyone involved.

NCAA RECRUIT TIPS: 7 STEPS TO A SCHOLARSHIP

Once you determine your non-negotiable decision factors (academic reputation, conference, location), keep it real with the coaches that are recruiting you. Believe me, if you don't tell them what your decision factors are, someone else around you will and it's best that you speak for yourself! Coaches are good with a player who can be up front with them and it's better they know your selection criteria from you directly instead of hearing it from a family member, high school or AAU coach or recruiting website who may misspeak for you.

Most coaches are professionals, they won't be mad at you. Disappointed for their programs, yes, but not mad if you can be up front with them. And most will even tell you to reach out to them down the road if you change your mind, they understand this may be a confusing and overwhelming experience for you and will pick up where they left off if you decide to re-open your recruitment down the road.

It's crucial you determine your decision factors and follow your heart! If you don't, coaches know you will be unhappy and eventually transfer from the program. They were all your age once! Keep it real with them and they will keep it real with you!

At the end of the day this is YOUR decision and you need to do what is in YOUR heart, do what makes YOU happy!

IT DOESN'T ALWAYS HAVE TO BE YOU AGAINST THE WORLD– STOP PUSHING THOSE CLOSE TO YOU AWAY. THERE ARE PEOPLE IN YOUR LIFE WHO WANT TO HELP.

10 TIPS FOR UNSIGNED SENIORS

#1 – Put together your Student-Athlete Resume

#2 – The #1 rule to remember is that coaches MUST see you play in order to be interested in recruiting you, either in person or on film. If you don't have any offers and nobody has come out to see you play, your main goal is to get coaches to evaluate your film.

#3 – When researching and contacting schools, you MUST figure out which assistant coach is in charge of recruiting your town, position, grade, etc. Each coaching staff splits recruiting responsibilities, so your priority is to find out which coach would be your 'recruiting coach.'

#4 – Talk to your prep coaches and see if they would be able to call some schools for you. What level do they think you would be able to play at? Do they know any college coaches who are at that level who may be able to give you a quick evaluation? Would your coaches be willing to make some cold calls for you?

#5 – Start contacting the local schools, schools within your state

#6 – If possible, try to evaluate which school lacks depth at your position. Recruiting decisions are based on timing, it will be difficult to get your foot in the door at a school that is stacked at your position. Coaches are much more likely to evaluate your film if they are in need of a player just like you.

#7 – Would you consider starting at a Junior College and transferring to a Division I or II school in a year or two? Many Division I and II programs put effort into scouting Junior College programs!

#8 – If you have no scholarship offers would you be interested in joining the team as a walk-on and work to secure non-athletic scholarships or student loans?

#9 – Register with the NCAA Eligibility Center if you haven't already. It is a MANDATORY step, and a sign of maturity to coaches that you've already begun the process.

#10 – Get a copy of your unofficial transcript ready as well as your SAT/ACT scores. Once coaches are interested in you, the next step will be to evaluate if you can qualify academically.

JUNIOR COLLEGE ROUTE

If you aren't getting the scholarship offers that you want or feel you should be getting by the end of your senior season, one of the final options to think about is to attend a Junior College for a year or two. Junior Colleges feed major FBS programs and hundreds of other schools every year with talented players who are able to step into starting positions. You are basically able to re-do the recruiting process once you are enrolled and competing at the Junior College level.

Aaron Rodgers, Deion Branch, Al Harris, Jeremy Shockey, Chris Johnson, Keshawn Johnson, Bryant McKinnie, Chad Ochocinco, Steve Smith, Duane Starks, Javon Walker and Cam Newton are just a few football players who went to Junior College at some point during their college career and went on to find tremendous success in college and the NFL. Many other NCAA teams recruit from Junior College programs as well.

Along with going the JuCo route for a year or two to basically re-do the recruiting process, some prep players must go that route in order to get the required grades and test scores needed before they can enroll in four-year institutions. Junior Colleges are definitely an option to consider if you feel you are a late-bloomer, had an injury or if you fell short academically.

NCAA RECRUIT TIPS: 7 STEPS TO A SCHOLARSHIP

I have worked for several major Division I coaches who put QUALITY attention into finding JuCo players. There are some coaches who specifically want to add one or two JuCo players to their roster each year and will scout them consistently.

Junior College players are important to NCAA programs that may have had many players transfer out, injuries or players who have exited school early for the draft. A team may be too heavy with a high percentage of freshman and incoming freshman on the roster and need a boost of older, more physically-ready players. Other programs may focus on Junior College players because they can't offer exciting locations or rankings—but they can offer players Division I starting jobs. JuCo players can come in to a program and make an immediate impact, the best ones are highly sought after by many elite FBS coaches.

More importantly, some Junior College players have been through their share of ups and downs and can be a more mature or goal-oriented than 17 or 18-year-old freshmen. JuCo players often appreciate the opportunity to play major college sports and are more disciplined than younger players. For many, this is their second chance and they are often more mature and willing to handle their business without being babysat compared to a player straight out of high school.

> **THERE COMES A TIME WHEN THERE'S NOTHING LEFT TO TALK ABOUT. IT'S STRITCLY ABOUT TAKING ACTION. DO WHAT YOU SAY YOU WILL DO.**

Junior Colleges have helped pave the way to an NCAA career for many players, so consider it an option if you feel it's your best opportunity to lead you to a more competitive school than you are being recruited by as a high school senior. Visit www.NJCAA.org for more information!

Reach out to JuCo coaches in the same ways you would contact NCAA coaches—call, email, send your film, have your prep coaches call.

WALK-ON OPPORTUNITIES

If you still dream of playing at the collegiate level and aren't getting scholarship offers or calls, evaluate if you would be able or willing to be a walk-on player. If your dream school has told you that they won't be able to offer you any scholarship money—would you be able to walk on? Is there a space for you and can you afford it?

@1001RecruitTips

30 TIPS FOR WALK-ONS: HOW TO MAKE THE TEAM AND TO EARN PLAYING TIME

BEFORE YOU MAKE THE TEAM

#1 – ASK HOW THE PROCESS WORKS: Walk-ons generally join the team in two ways, either as a preferred walk-on or through a tryout. A preferred walk-on doesn't have to tryout—they are borderline offers, favors for influential people or players from successful prep programs. Players that must tryout (MUST already be enrolled in classes at that university), complete compliance paperwork, get a physical and show up to the open tryout on a select date. You may need to weigh out your options after speaking with the schools that you are interested in to see which ones may be your best chance to make the team, it's not guaranteed and the spaces are extremely competitive. See how the process works at each school.

#2 – OTHER SCHOLARSHIPS AND LOANS: Apply for other scholarships (academic, service, legacy, major) and student loans. Nearly every other college student has to work to secure their scholarships and loans, so can you!

#3 – SEND HIGHLIGHT VIDEO: Walk-on positions are just as competitive to get as scholarship spots, so you can approach the coaches in the same way—they need to see you play. Organize your highlight video and your Student-Athlete Resume, contact the school, find out who the 'Walk-On Coordinator' is and forward your information to them for review. Follow-up within a week or two!

#4 – DO THEY NEED YOUR POSITION: Like scholarship spots, walk-on positions are usually slotted for a particular position or two that the team is lacking depth in. Again, if they are stacked at your position, they aren't likely to add you, choosing another player who can help at a position of need instead. Try back again in a year, and maybe even the next year.

#5 – WHAT ARE THEY LOOKING FOR: When you speak with the Walk-On Coordinator, ask them specifically what they are looking for—size, speed, grades, campus leadership? Each coach and program is looking to add something different—ask them specifically what type of players they need?

#6 – ASK FOR DRILLS: When you speak with the Walk-On Coordinator, ask them for drills, or ask your potential position coach for a few key drills. You can call or email for this information, or if you are already enrolled, stop by the office. It shows you are going above and beyond and willing to do the extra work to be prepared for your tryout. It won't guarantee you a spot (heck, you may not even get any sample drills), but it will show your work ethic and your desire to be prepared.

#7 – TRAIN: Prepare, prepare, prepare! Many players come out and haven't been putting in the consistent work that the current players have been putting in. Get up early and run, make strides in the weight room. Coaches are looking for skill, size and speed. Those are three ways you can get your foot in the door. Work on your position-specific drills, be in the best shape possible and train just as hard as the current scholarship athletes are training! Focus on improving skill, size and speed!

NCAA RECRUIT TIPS: 7 STEPS TO A SCHOLARSHIP

#8 – HAVE YOUR COACHES CALL: Ask your prep coaches to make a call to the coaches or Director of Operations to find out how the process works, what they are looking for and how you can secure a preferred walk-on spot or tryout. In some cases, your coach may be able to get more info that you can get.

#9 – ATTEND SUMMER CAMP: Entering your senior year of high school, if you haven't had much interest, particularly in your dream school, considering participating in their summer camp. It gives you a few days to network with the coaches and for them to get a chance to see you play. Coaches normally add a few players to their recruiting watch lists based off working with them in camp and after evaluating their size, skill and speed in person. You may not be scholarship-ready but you may be able to network with them and earn a walk-on spot. If you have a select school in mind, this is a great opportunity to get your foot in the door to try to earn a preferred walk-on slot. The earlier the better.

#10 – OFFER TO WORK CAMPS: If you are already enrolled at the university, check with the Camp Director or the Director of Operations in the spring and submit a resume or letter of interest, offering to work summer camps. These part-time positions may be on a week-by-week basis or may last throughout several weeks during the summer. Although they often pay, be willing to negotiate to volunteer if there are no extra positions available. Anything you can do to get your foot in the door, networking with the coaches and decision-makers, will give them a chance to see your work ethic and passion. You may be coaching elementary students or filling up the Gatorade coolers, but this can be an audition to show the coaches how hard you are willing to work to be a part of the program and get inside information on what skills they are looking for, what drills you can be working on and what sizes/speeds coaches are looking to bring in. Again, you might not make the team on the first try but at least they'll be able to put a name with a face and that always helps.

#11 – MULTIPLE TRY-OUTS: If at first you don't succeed, try... try again! I've been a part of many teams where a player eventually made the squad after trying out more than one time. If you don't make the cut the first year (don't play a position of need, aren't big or fast enough) then use that year to keep training. It is not uncommon for players to have to try out more than once to be able to make the team. Humble yourself and keep showing up!

#12 – STUDENT MANAGER: A similar idea to working camps. Any way you can get your foot in the door, networking with the coaches, understanding what they are looking for, seeing first-hand how hard the players work and what drills they participate in will only help you. It's not uncommon for a walk-on to make the team after working for a year or two as a manager. If you work hard, are willing to do anything to help the team (laundry, class checks, field set-up) on that level, coaches will take your work ethic into consideration as they are making their decisions. You will have an edge over other candidates who they have no relationship with.

#13 – ACADEMICS COUNT: Most walk-ons have outstanding grades, and their academic standing can help boost the team's overall GPA and academic standing. Coaches sometimes have enough trouble monitoring their scholarship players and their grades, they will not tolerate a walk-on player who isn't pulling their weight in the classroom. Don't let your academic standing be a reason to eliminate you from consideration, coaches are looking to add scholars and leaders, not just average students!

#14 – HOW CAN YOU BRING VALUE TO THE TEAM: Similar to scholarship players, what can you do to separate yourself and bring value to the team? Are you a top scholar, a student leader, a special teams superstar, an undersized speedster, someone who will take scout team extremely seriously? Can you be the best rebounder on the court? Find a way to get an edge—through leadership, academics, toughness or attitude. What is the team lacking, how can you become a specialist at that skill?

#15 – LOCAL PRODUCT: If playing for your hometown team is your dream, guess what—you actually have a slight advantage over other potential walk-ons. Coaches LOVE adding a local player or two who was a great hometown player in the area who may be choosing to stay closer to home, who is a life-long fan and who has local following. Contact the coaches or have your prep coach contact the Walk-On Coordinator during your junior or senior year and get the conversation going!

Coaches are likely open to it, especially if you were a great player and leader for your high school!

YOU MAKE THE TEAM, HOW TO EARN PLAYING TIME:

#16 – PLAYBOOK, FILM JUNKIE: Earn the respect of your coaches and teammates by knowing the playbook better than any other player and by becoming a filmroom junkie. Although you may not be as naturally talented as other scholarship players, understanding the playbook backwards and forwards can only help you, and can help you assist your coaches and teammates during games. Many walk-ons become future coaches, and that begins with learning the importance of having a high IQ in your sport in terms of strategy, core philosophy and personnel. Being one of the smartest and most prepared players in the meeting room will help you get on the field at some point. Film will also give you an advantage, so once you understand how to get the most of it and you will be able to anticipate plays better in live games, you may pick up on tendencies quickly and be able to communicate those to your coaches or teammates. This can be one of your best angles to get some playing time!

#17 – MAKE TEAMMATES BETTER: Be serious in meetings and during practice on scout team, do whatever you can do to make your teammates better. Don't be frustrated as a player on scout team, take great pride in it, it IS your way to help the team! The more prepared they are, the more reps they are able to get in during practice, the more successful they are likely to be. Initiate extra reps after practice with your teammates, offer to help, stay late or come in on off days to help the starters! You will be improving as well and getting a step closer to some playing time!

#18 – FIRST THERE, LAST TO LEAVE: Coaches appreciate players who are ready to come to work every day. A key way to earn respect is by being the first player there and the last player to leave. Get in extra reps for yourself, or as mentioned above, help make the starters better by initiating extra reps after practice or on off days. Coaches will take notice! Those 15 or 30 extra minutes of drills will add up over the season and you will become a better player. Ask your coach for drills that you need work on and can do on your own, they love nothing more than players who take initiative to get better!

NCAA RECRUIT TIPS: 7 STEPS TO A SCHOLARSHIP

#19 – WAIT FOR CHANCE: A lot of walk-ons may go into the process thinking that playing time in-game is your chance. That's going to be a goal you will work towards down the road. Realize that scout team IS your chance. The role of scout team is very important to coaches, and can make a difference in the success of the team. Take pride and ownership of your unit, just as you would of your position group if you were a starter. Keep it competitive versus first and second teamers. Play fundamentally sound, if coaches can trust you in practice to not make careless mistakes they'll be more likely to trust you in game situations! Your first goal is to be the most outstanding scout team player and getting playing time in that way. Many walk-ons may not even see practice time, let alone game time.

Realize that this is your first goal! The better you do preparing the team through scout team, the more likely your coaches will trust you in live game situations down the road!

#20 – DO WHATEVER YOU CAN TO MAKE A DIFFERENCE: A lot of walk-ons join the team trying to be 'too cool.' They are sometimes bigger divas than the top recruits. Humble yourself, keep a positive attitude and do whatever you can do for your teammates and coaches to be able to make a difference. Drop the diva attitude, a humble attitude will get you much, much further!

#21 – CONSISTENT AND DEPENDABLE: Another thing coaches are looking for are players who are consistent and dependable—in everything that they do. In your unit, if you can be the player who provides consistency, stability and reliability to the team, you will earn your coaches respect. Take it a step further, once you are part of the team and hanging out with the other players outside of the facility, be the voice of reason in situations where starters and scholarship players may need guidance. If you are around negative situations or altercations, help remove the starters and scholarship players from the environment—never be the one who escalates it. You will be off the roster immediately, be the 'voice of reason' when your coaches aren't around.

#22 – DO THE DIRTY WORK: Special teams, rebounding, blocking, toughness, extra work.... Again, everyone wants to be the leading scorer, rusher, playmaker but there are key skills that COACHES are looking for that can help win games. They may not get the glory or the fans, but they are critical skills in helping the team win. Do those tasks that most other players think they are too good for— blocking, rebounding, cheerleading from the bench, running scout team. Get in there and get your jersey dirty. Make a difference in those skills that actually help change the game.

#23 – THERE FOR THE RIGHT REASONS: A key piece of advice that I give elite scholarship athletes is "Chase greatness and everything else will come." This applies to walk-ons as well. Over the years I've noticed that a good percentage of walk-ons are 'in it' for the wrong reasons, they aren't necessarily there for the love of the game. Those players never last or see playing time, the walk-ons who are eventually put in a position to earn playing time are the ones who are chasing GREATNESS first— not the opposite sex, media, popularity or any of the other fringe benefits. Be there for the right reason—the love of the game and your school—and you'll succeed!

#24 – BIGGEST CHEERLEADER: It cannot be stated enough how important ENERGY and MOMENTUM can help your team. As a walk-on, you may not see much playing time but you do play a major role during competitions. Clap it up— when things are going good, when the team is facing sudden change or adversity or when the game is on the line. Even when a key player makes a critical mistake, be the first one over to tell them to keep their head up and that they'll make the play next time. Keep your teammates confident and focused and bring the energy to the sideline! In and out of quarters or halftime, between time-outs—CLAP IT UP! That is your job, and YES, it can help win!

#25 – DON'T HARASS STAFF: Many walk-ons are some of the most popular and fun players on the team, they're happy to be there. Other walk-ons think they have to be DEMANDING in order to earn respect. I've come across my fair share of walk-ons who always tried to demand extra equipment, gear, exceptions and it's something coaches don't want to hear about. Treat your academic counselors, equipment managers, trainers and other staff with respect or you could find yourself cut from the roster for having a disrespecting attitude. You can't demand respect, go earn it.

#26 – MENTOR YOUNGER PLAYERS: Once you are on the team and a veteran, take some of the freshmen under your wing, especially at your position. Coaches are always looking for leaders within the team, and you will be helping your position out if you can help mentor a rookie and show them the ropes, on and off- campus. Tips for class, laundry, cooking, rides, breaking the ice...

#27 – HELP WITH RECRUITING: On official visit weekends, recruits are paired up with hosts, and there are some occasions where coaches would pair up a player with a walk-on, they are at times the funniest or most personable players on the team. They may actually have more passion or school spirit, and it can be infectious! Anything you can do to help the team, including hosting a prospect or helping during official visit weekends will be a help to your coaches.

#28 – PARENTS: Coaches don't usually respond well when parents call to complain about playing time or petty stuff. They ESPECIALLY don't like it if it's for a walk-on, particularly if you aren't a key scout team or special teams player. In my experience, we once had a parent who constantly complained that their walk-on son should be starting ahead of the current starter... a player who would go on to win multiple Super Bowl Championships as a starter. Appreciate your opportunity and keep the complaints about playing time to a minimum. Champions never complain their way out of a problem, they work their way out!

#29 – NEVER EMBARRASS THE TEAM OR THE COACHES: Especially in the newspapers—arrests or incidents with the police will be another quick way to find yourself off the team. Again, you may not even have the opportunity to give the coaches your side of the story if there is a pattern of bad behavior or legal incidents. Some coaches tolerate legal issues with scholarship players and may give them second or third chances but most won't tolerate issues with walk-ons. You are there to bring positive light to the program, never negative attention!

#30 – HAVE FUN: Most importantly, HAVE FUN! Playing at the collegiate level, in the sport that you love, will be a life-changing experience. To many walk-ons, it's an experience they'd actually pay for at the end of the day. I'd give up many things to go back to those four seasons in undergrad with my team! If every other regular student has to find scholarships or loans or depend on their family, then you are simply doing the same thing and getting the chance to live out your dream—being part of your college team! Enjoy it!

DO WALK-ONS EVER EARN SCHOLARSHIP MONEY?

If you are a contributing member of the team who works their way into a starting position or who makes major contributions in-games and has earned a significant role with consistent playing time, there is a good chance your coach may award you with some scholarship money as a senior or junior — but it's not guaranteed.

Making the team as a walk-on gets your foot in the door, it gets you a shot at practice. Treat practice as your games and realize that any reps that you get are critical, treat them with respect and make the most of them. If you are on scout team, focus on doing whatever you can to prepare the starters.

> "LIFE IS NEVER GONNA GET EASIER, BUT EVERY DAY I MUST FIND A WAY TO GET STRONGER."

Coaches are looking for "difference makers" who can help them win games. While most players are just trying to get the ball or spotlight, focus on what you can become a specialist at that can help your team win games—special teams, rebounding, blocking, ball security, steals, etc. You may never be the leading scorer but you can become the best blocker, toughest rebounder or difference-maker on special teams—and those advantages and strengths you can bring to your team can help you earn a scholarship or starting job.

Coaches love players who play great fundamentals, who hustle and who are tough. No matter your size, skill or speed—these are traits you can always work on. Focus on your fundamentals, toughness and ALWAYS hustle. Have no off-field issues (academic, attitude, legal) and HUSTLE!

HOW TO HELP PAY FOR SCHOOL OUTSIDE OF ATHLETIC SCHOLARSHIPS

Hundreds of thousands of student-athletes are lucky enough to earn athletic scholarships... but millions of other students each year are not, and must find ways to pay for their college education! Tuition, university fees, room and board, academic supplies, books and living expenses add up quickly!

Here are some ways to help cover expenses for a college education, learn more at www.studentaid.ed.gov/sa/:

- Federal Work Study (Jobs)

- Scholarships
    o Academic
    o Merit – Artistic, Extracurricular, Community Service-based aid
    o Need-based
    o Student-Specific (gender, race, religion, family/medical history and other factors)
    o Career-Specific (based on your choice of major or field of interest)
    o College-Specific

- Federal Student Aid

    o Grants/Scholarships
        > Federal Pell Grant
        > FSEOG (Grants)
        > TEACH Grants
        > Iraq/Afghanistan Service Grant
        > Aid for Military Families

    o Loans
        > Subsidized and Unsubsidized Loans
        > PLUS Loans
        > Perkins Loans
        > Private Loans

Shop around! Tuition's vary greatly from school-to-school, schools are able to offer a variety of different aid packages and most schools charge higher rates for out-of-state students. Sit down with your family and determine a budget, and begin the paperwork for other aid.

For more information, visit WWW.STUDENTAID.ED.GOV/SA/ on the above financial aid options!

DEALING WITH ISSUES WITH THE NCAA

The NCAA and their rules and member institutions make up a very complex and powerful world. As you are submitting information to the NCAA Eligibility Center and working towards admission and enrollment to your chosen university you may encounter setbacks. You may have academic credit deficiencies, questions and investigations into your amateur status, flagged SAT/ACT scores, problems with your transcripts... the NCAA problems that players can run into are limitless.

The #1 rule to remember during this time is to just be honest, tell the truth. If the NCAA catches you in a lie, your shot is over. They take their time, attempt to get all of the information and rarely rush to a decision. It's best to take a deep breath, tell the truth and wait out a decision. Even if you are guilty on some level and tell the truth, you may face reinstatement or minor punishments. If you are guilty and lie about it, they are doing their investigations interviewing several other people involved in the situation and can permanently end your career if they come to the conclusion that you are lying.

I've worked with a handful of players and coaches who were in the center of NCAA investigations—some minor and some that became national news. In high profile cases, the public perception is that players and coaches are guilty until proven innocent. It's not fair, but it is the case. That's why it's best to be honest, keep a low profile and wait on the investigation to run its course.

PLAN TO TRANSFER IN A YEAR OR TWO TO JUMP TO A HIGHER DIVISION

Does your plan include signing with a school, and then jumping ship in a year or two to greener pastures? Is it possible, yes. Is it your best option, probably not.

If you are considering this option, you are likely not getting the offers that you are interested in, or you are a late bloomer. Both are situations that happen to a lot of college athletes, relax.

An alternative to trying to work off this plan would be to start at a Junior College for a year or two, you can basically re-do the recruiting process and transfer to a four-year institution. It's true—college coaches, especially Division I coaches, begin evaluating players younger and younger, and if you are a late bloomer or were dealing with off-the-field issues, you may not be getting the offers and recruitment that you think you deserve. Junior College opportunities give you the chance to start over, give you another year to improve and get bigger, and see if a better opportunity comes along—and many JuCos offer athletic scholarship aid.

It's also important to note, that all that glitters is not gold. I've worked with small programs, operating on nickel and dime budgets and I've worked among the best with near limitless budgets... you can build great friendships and make life-long memories at many schools. Don't limit yourself to only Division I schools, you can be missing out on scholarship money and the overall college experience.

Yes, transfers happen to nearly every team in the country. You may get there and the fit may just not be right, or your relationship with your coach may just not be working for you. You may have new family issues at home and would be more comfortable at a school within an hour or two from your hometown. Transferring is an option, but should be part of your overall plan. Coaches and teammates put time and effort into building their program, it's not good to take advantage of that and go chasing after "something better." Remember the old saying, "the grass isn't always greener on the other side."

WHAT IF AN INJURY INTERRUPTS MY CAREER
One of the toughest adversities all athletes face are injuries, particularly season or career-ending injuries. From my experiences, they are much tougher mentally on most players than physically.

From a recruiting standpoint, not all season-ending injuries will effect your potential to earn a scholarship. From my experiences, college coaches will often stick by injured players and continue to recruit and evaluate them, possibly even offer them. If you already have scholarship offers, an injury doesn't necessarily mean that they will be pulled.

The toughest situation is for those players who are seniors and still working towards getting offers, if you find yourself in this situation you will just need to get more creative and more aggressive. The key to success in this situation is to remain mentally tough. You must keep your confidence, develop other aspects of your game, become a master of the playbook. If you are a basketball player who breaks their leg—get in the job, get someone to help rebound for you, and get shots up! If you break your right hand, get in the gym and learn to shoot with your left hand, work on your quickness, vertical and conditioning.

If you are an unsigned senior, you must continue to pound the pavement, work the phones, send your highlights and follow-up. You may have to go to prep school, Junior College or a much less competitive program.

You must find a way to OVERCOME. You must work towards this every day. You must stay positive! Remember—you always have options, even if you may not see them in the moment.

NCAA RECRUIT TIPS: 7 STEPS TO A SCHOLARSHIP

WAYS TO ADDRESS ISSUES WITH YOUR CHILD'S COACH

I often hear the phrase, "My coach is against me," or "My child's coach shows favoritism towards other players." Yes, favoritism does sometimes happen and yes, almost every player feels their coach is against them at some point. (These are intended for college-aged players but some points also apply to youth sports...)

Before your child makes the final decision to quit or transfer to another university, put some thought into these points:

#1- You're not going to win every battle, it's just not realistic to think you will always get your way with your child's coach. If you do, your child isn't playing for a quality coach or you are in the wrong profession!

#2- Understand that you run your house one way, and coaches have the authority to run their 'house' their way. Very few coaches are going to drastically change their approach so it's often their way, or the highway when it comes to player-coach disagreements. It's up to the Athletic Director to decide if the coach is running their program in an acceptable way. Then, it's up to your child (and family) to decide if they want to be a part of it

#3- Coaches mindset is to do what is best for the PROGRAM and TEAM. Your job as a parent has always been to do what is best for your CHILD. Those are two different sets of priorities that are often on different timelines and paces. It takes time for athletes to develop, coaches understand it's a process while some parents expect miracles overnight.

#4- To avoid issues, it's best to have an open relationship with your child's coaches—not just the head coach but assistant coaches too. Tell them to feel free to call you and keep you up-to-date on any problems your child is having. Without communication, your first sign of trouble may be too late. Many problems can be resolved if everyone communicates.

#5- Understand that coaches want to win just as much as anyone else—their job actually depends on it. Therefore, they're going to play the best option available. Also understand most coaches would "rather be 1 week late than 1 week early" in terms of when to give an athlete playing time or a starting job. They would rather KNOW the player is ready than to THINK the player is ready if there is quality depth at that position.

#6- Many players face the same problems that affect their happiness and/or playing time. Ask your child's coach if they know the root of the problem:
   – Often issues with playing time are the result of players being less skilled, less conditioned, players with negative attitudes, tardiness, class attendance problems or issues with practice, weights or study hall

– Many issues also stem from personal problems that players may be going through: family stress, health problems, relationship issues, stress, money stress, a death in the family, etc.

#7- Threatening or insulting your child's coach rarely works—You will never bully them into changing their mind so save your time.

#8- From a coaches' standpoint, many playing time issues other than talent level stem from a lack of maturity. You may not see it at home, immaturity may rise to the top once players are in competitive or pressure situations.

> **SUCCESSFUL PEOPLE KNOW THIS: YOU CAN'T COMPLAIN YOUR WAY OUT OF YOUR PROBLEMS-- YOU HAVE TO WORK YOUR WAY OUT!**

#9- Understand that rosters change all the time. Your child will have opportunities—they just may take more time than expected. Playing time changes from player-to-player at many positions throughout the year due to suspensions, academic issues, injuries, etc.

#10- YOUR JOB as a parent is to help your children develop patience. The younger they learn this, the better they will handle disappointments on the field and in life. Your child's freshman year of college (or high school) is not the time to introduce them to the concepts of patience and having a strong work ethic!

#11- Negative attitudes from many players stem from sources outside of their team: parents, hometown friends, high school coaches and teammates are always asking, "Why aren't you playing yet?" Eliminate this pressure! Do not feed your child's negative attitude with even more negativity or pressure about playing time.

#12- Instead of always telling your child that their coach is "not fair," tell them to "work a little harder."

#13- Every year I have worked with a player who has transferred and within the year, a spot opened up, a spot they could have easily stepped in to. Many teams lack depth, and spots open up every day, every year. Teach your children a strong work ethic and patience.

#14- In some cases, there are equally talented and capable players at the same position. There are only so many positions on the field/court. Sometimes coaches can rotate players at that position successful to share playing time but alternating players often can disrupt team chemistry. Players need stability on the court/field, so there are times when a player may have to wait longer for their opportunity, even if they are equally as talented as the starter in front of them.

NCAA RECRUIT TIPS: 7 STEPS TO A SCHOLARSHIP

#15- Many historically great players didn't earn starting jobs until their junior or senior year! Players aren't failures if they aren't starting as freshmen or sophomores. Focus on how your children can DEVELOP throughout their college career—they have four or five (or even sometimes six) years to develop into a great, contributing player. Remember—to be a part of a team with great depth is a gift and will likely get them closer to a championship and learning what it takes to win and develop strong teamwork skills.

REMEMBER – lessons learned in youth and college sports translate to your child's adult life. They are learning more than just Xs and Os—they are learning how to deal with disappointment and adversity while developing a work ethic, competitive drive and relentless attitude that they can carry over into business and their professional and family life. Egos must be kept in check!

ACTION STEPS: IF PLAN 'A' ISN'T WORKING

- **JUNIOR COLLEGE ROUTE:** IF YOU THINK THAT YOU COULD USE ANOTHER YEAR OR TWO OF PHYSICAL OR ACADEMIC IMPROVEMENTS IN ORDER TO BE RECRUITED BY AN NCAA PROGRAM, CONSIDER STARTING YOUR COLLEGIATE CAREER AT A JUNIOR COLLEGE. APPROACH COACHES IN THE SAME WAY THAT YOU WOULD APPROACH NCAA COACHES, WITH FILM AND YOUR STUDENT-ATHLETE RESUME. DEVELOP YOUR TARGET LIST OF JUCO PROGRAMS THAT ARE COMPETITIVE OR NEARBY, AND WORK THROUGH THAT LIST COMMUNICATING WITH THEIR COACHES.

- **WALK-ON OPPORTUNITIES:** IF YOU ARE SET ON ATTENDING A SPECIFIC SCHOOL AND ARE NOT GETTING CONSIDERED FOR A SCHOLARSHIP, WOULD YOU BE INTERESTED IN JOINING THE TEAM AS A WALK-ON? IF SO, BEGIN REACHING OUT TO THAT SCHOOL WITH OUR 30 TIPS TO MAKE THE TEAM AS A WALK-ON (PAGE 159). MANY OF THESE SPOTS ARE JUST AS COMPETITIVE AS SCHOLARSHIP SPOTS, SO DON'T WAIT UNTIL YOU ENROLL TO BEGIN HAVING THESE CONVERSATIONS! APPROACH COACHES IN THE SAME WAY WITH YOUR VIDEO AND STUDENT-ATHLETE RESUME.

- **OVERCOMING INJURIES:** CONTINUE TO WORK TOWARDS YOUR SCHOLARSHIP GOALS, EVEN IF YOU HAVE FACED A RECENT INJURY, EVEN SEASON-ENDING INJURY. FOR MANY PLAYERS, OVERCOMING AN INJURY CAN BE TOUGHER MENTALLY THAN PHYSICALLY. DON'T LET DOUBT CREEP IN, REHAB AS INSTRUCTED AND CONTINUE TO IMPROVE IN OTHER AREAS THAT YOU CAN WORK ON WHILE INJURED. THERE ARE ALWAYS WAYS TO IMPROVE – EVEN THROUGH SETBACKS!

- **IMPROVING MENTAL TOUGHNESS:** DEVELOP A MANTRA OR SAYING THAT YOU CAN REPEAT TO YOURSELF WHEN TIMES GET TOUGH, BECAUSE THEY UNDOUBTEDLY WILL GET TOUGH! YOU'LL HAVE TO LEARN TO STOP LETTING DOUBTS CREEP INTO YOUR MIND, YOU'LL HAVE TO LEARN TO WORK THROUGH THE ANXIETY. IF PLAYING COLLEGE SPORTS WAS THAT EASY, THERE WOULD BE MILLIONS OF OTHER ATHLETES OUT THERE DOING IT. YOU'RE GOING TO HAVE TO FIGHT FOR THE OPPORTUNITY, IF YOU REALLY WANT ONE! IT STARTS WITH DEVELOPING A WINNING ATTITUDE AND BECOMING A MENTALLY TOUGH PLAYER!

MY MANTRA FOR OVERCOMING TOUGH TIMES:

_____

_____

_____

- **TIPS FOR UNSIGNED SENIORS:** IF A SENIOR, WHICH WAYS CAN YOU USE "10 TIPS FOR UNSIGNED SENIORS" CAN YOU USE TO FIND WAYS TO GET EVALUATED AND RECRUITED? MAKE A LIST OF THE TOP 3 WAYS THAT YOU CAN REALISTICALLY GET YOUR NAME OUT THERE, THE QUICKEST AND MOST EFFICIENT WAY POSSIBLE. AFTER YOU'VE EXHAUSTED THOSE THREE AVENUES, CONTINUE THROUGH THE LIST WITH THE BEST WAYS YOU CAN GAIN EXPOSURE AND EVALUATIONS.

NCAA RECRUIT TIPS: 7 STEPS TO A SCHOLARSHIP

STEP #7
REMAIN IN CONTROL

"Don't follow the crowd, let the crowd follow you."
– MARGARET THATCHER

"In order to be a leader, you don't blame people. You solve problems. Take some ownership of your issues."
– MARCUS LEMONIS

"You can't empower people who are dependent."
– STEPHEN R. COVEY

"Become the kind of leader that people would follow voluntarily, even if you had no title or position."
– BRIAN TRACY

NEVER PUT AN EXPIRATION DATE ON YOUR DREAMS
To some the recruiting process will be more than frustrating and to some, the rejection and feedback (or lack of response) may be too much.

Remember—you just need to find that ONE coaching staff who believes in you, not earn 50 scholarship offers from schools across the country. You may not even start (or finish) as a scholarship player—but the goal of playing college athletics on any level is something you should never give up on! I'm here to tell you : NEVER PUT AN EXPIRATION DATE ON YOUR DREAMS! You may have to start out at a Junior College, or as a walk-on with no scholarship. You may have to try out to be a walk-on two or three times. You may never see game action until your senior year... you may never hear the announcer call your name during starting lineups... BUT, what you will have is a lifetime of memories and most likely, a lifetime of lessons.

Along with the wins, the scholarship money and maybe even the TV time... college athletics are more about the relationships with your teammates, coaches and university, about the memories and about the lessons you've learned that will help you in your adult life.

You must WORK for what you want, stay positive in your persistence and always keep the dream alive, no matter what anyone says!

ALWAYS REMAIN IN CONTROL
Your dream is something that you will have to fight for, live for and chase on a daily basis. Don't ever take your foot off the gas, when positive things begin happening for you is when you need to hit the gas even harder. You will have doors slammed in your face and you will likely be underestimated—setbacks that all successful people and champions have faced. You must have a plan, a passion and a purpose and I have hoped to draw that out of you throughout this book.

It's important to have a dream, chase the goals that everyone tells you that you will never achieve and to keep believing—but it's equally as important to have a solid back- up plan. You never want to leave any offers or opportunities on the table. Remember—no school will ever justify how talented you are, never base your value as a person on who has offered you—you are worth way more than that!

I am here to tell you that no matter what, YOU are the only person who will stop yourself. Not your coaches, your parents, your teammates or your grades. Whenever you feel powerless (which you will at some point, we all do), remember that you always have the power to get an extra workout in, the power to go for a run, the power to be patient, the power to study harder, the power to work harder, to try again and to always have control of your attitude. If you 'find a way' in everything you do, good things start happening!

FIND a way, MAKE a way, BE RELENTLESS and don't you EVER quit on yourself—no matter how many people try to stand in your way!

Good luck—see you at the finish line.

KEEP CONSTANT, CONSISTENT, POSITIVE AND UNCONDITIONAL FAITH IN YOURSELF!

SIGNED, SEALED & DELIVERED: ADVICE FOR SCHOLARSHIP SIGNEES AND INVITED WALK-ONS

The NLI is signed! But... this is not the end of the process for you— it's just the beginning:

#1– No matter how talented you are, you didn't get to this point alone. Now is the time to thank your parents, siblings, coaches, family members, mentors, teammates and friends who have helped and supported you along the way.

#2– No matter how long you've been wanting to move far, far away and leave everyone behind... you WILL get homesick! Don't burn too many bridges on your way out, you'll be back!

#3– Everything that the sweet-talking coaches have told you to this point about starting jobs and playing time... throw it out the window. You're going to have to earn playing time and a starting job... and they may not come for a couple years.

#4– When you think back in 20 years, you won't remember what type of gear you got, how many times you were on TV, what kind of media hype you got. All you will remember are the relationships with your teammates and coaches.

#5– Whether you are eating a steak on charter flights, flying all around the country or bussing for eight hours and eating boxed lunches on road trips – these are the memories you will remember years from now! Being a part of any college team is a blessing!

#6– The 'Golden Rules' for freshmen:
 – Be 5-10 minutes early for everything (class, practice, weights, meeting, treatment, study hall)
 – Just do what is asked of you the first time
 – Chase greatness and the rest (media attention, popularity, hype) will follow. Players who chase everything else first never find true success

#7– Many of you will end up redshirting or riding the bench next year. No matter what a coach tells you during the recruiting process, they really don't 100% know where

NCAA RECRUIT TIPS: 7 STEPS TO A SCHOLARSHIP

you will fit in on the depth chart until after pre-season workouts are over. Greatness takes time and it's not about how quickly you become a starter, it's about what you accomplish over your career!

#8– Your social media not only has your name attached to it but also "student-athlete at _____ University" behind it now! Know that your tweets and pics can end up on ESPN, on the Athletic Director's desk, in your head coaches' texts messages or opponents' lockerroom within minutes.

#9– There are eyes and ears all over campus and town and nearly anything negative that you do will get back to your coaches. Once on a university campus, you can't hide.

#10– The people who will be most involved in your transition when you arrive on campus are your position coach, strength coach, academic counselor and athletic trainer. Get to know them, talk to them on a personal level and appreciate them!

#11– There is a good chance your head coach or the coach who recruited you won't be there during your entire career. Changes will happen on the staff every year, so your attitude will determine who well you handle these changes.

#12– You may be on your own for the first time in your life and facing adult decisions – are you ready to become a parent? I've worked with athletes almost every year who are thrust into parenthood – make your choices wisely!

#13– Some of the most selfish people I know were in TEAM situations. It's not always about you! Trust me, it's much more fun to win as a team than to be a superstar on a losing team!

#14– Where you are rated RIGHT NOW plays no role in how you'll finish your college career – high or low.

#15– No one player, no one person is bigger than the university. If you can't follow university rules and find yourself in trouble – understand they will never sacrifice the college's reputation for you. And sometimes you may not even get the chance to explain yourself!

#16– No matter how frustrated you may get, realize that you are one of the few who is lucky enough to graduate college debt-free!

#17– How you handle winning and losing will carry over to your adult life. Learning how to handle adversity on the field/court will help you as an adult with family, career and money issues.

#18– Take the time to just enjoy being a college kid! Enjoy the times in the dorms, study groups, dining hall, student activities, class, other sporting events. Be a regular student!

#19– Some of you 5-star athletes will never make a significant impact on your team because you lack a 5-star work ethic! At the college level, it's not just good enough to be talented – you must WORK!

#20- Some of you will get injured. This could all end tomorrow… so ENJOY IT!

#21- Don't be so hard on yourself! This is supposed to be fun, right?!?! Believe in yourself and keep working.

WHAT TO EXPECT: 14 TIPS FOR YOUR FIRST MONTH ON CAMPUS AS A COLLEGIATE STUDENT-ATHLETE

As an athlete, let your actions speak louder than your words! College coaches make a million promises during the recruiting process, understand it won't be as easy for you as they've made it sound. There will be adjustments and tough times, but they brought you there for a reason and believe in you!

Some first year tips for your first year on campus…

#1- TIME MANAGEMENT will be the toughest obstacle off-the-field you experience when you arrive on campus. Between class, practice, homework, games, study hall, travel, meals, treatment, weight training, film review, position meetings and team meetings you will be scheduled down to the minute, basically from sun up to sun down. Having a social life is a major part of the entire college experience and an aspect of your life that will have time limits, especially your freshman year while you are learning to balance everything. You need to prioritize your tasks and have good time management skills in order to manage and enjoy it all. Eliminating drama is a key part of time management! (See page 135).

#2- HAVE A GREAT ATTITUDE, be someone that your teammates and coaches want to be around. Too many freshmen get frustrated and bitter too quickly over playing time issues – most often, even before pre-season camp is over. This is a process, enjoy the ride. Your freshman year will be over quick! It's not about how quickly you start your career, but what you are able to accomplish over your entire career. Have a great attitude while developing during your first year as a collegiate athlete!

#3- BE ON TIME — better yet, show up 5-10 minutes early for all mandatory activities! Coaches are molding you to follow all instructions, so if you are late for class, practice, meetings, treatment or team travel, expect punishments. Punishments will only make your schedule even tighter, so it's best to just be on time! In most programs, tardiness or unexcused absences are the reasons most freshman face internal punishments! BE ON TIME, coaches will be extra strict during your first semester on campus! Get an alarm clock, partner with your teammates to make sure everyone is awake and on the way to early workouts. Even if you are going to be just a few minutes late—call or text your coaches to let them know that you are on the way.

#4- UNDERSTAND THERE ARE OPPORTUNITIES EVERY DAY! Practice is your biggest opportunity, along with understanding the playbook, film review, position meetings. Learn the system and develop your position skills—and don't feel overlooked if you aren't starting or playing a ton of minutes (or at all) yet. Get an advantage with the Xs and Os. Learn to do things your head coach's way! Rather focusing just on playing time and stats, focus on EVERY opportunity you have to showcase your skills.

NCAA RECRUIT TIPS: 7 STEPS TO A SCHOLARSHIP

#5- THE FILM DOESN'T LIE, let it be a great reflection of your skills, speed and maturity. Coaches watch how you behave on the sideline—be about business when at practice and meetings, even if you are on the sideline or third-string. Coaches watch everyone, all the time, and how you behave when you think they aren't watching does play a role in their overall picture of your maturity.

#6- DO THE DIRTY WORK OTHERS WON'T. Rebounds, blocking, helping set the play up, etc. Players worry about stats, starts and how many touches they get—what can you do without the ball in your hand to help the team? Ask your coaches! If you aren't playing, always have a positive energy on the sideline and be your team's biggest cheerleader. There are always ways you can help your team—be a positive force any way that you can.

#7- GET THE CELL PHONE NUMBERS of your position coach, head coach, Director of Operations, trainer, academic advisor, strength coach, sports information contact and grad assistants. Chances are, something urgent will come up during your first weeks on campus and you will need to get ahold of someone on staff after hours. Know how to get ahold of key staff quickly.

#8- PREPARE YOURSELF TO BE CHALLENGED MORE THAN YOU EVER HAVE BEEN IN YOUR ENTIRE ATHLETIC CAREER. Many freshman come in with high expectations, confidence, big personal goals and anxiety about playing time and starting jobs. As long as you understand that you will likely be challenged more than you ever have before, that it WON'T be as easy as you think it will be and that greatness is a process—don't be so hard on yourself. Enjoy your freshman year, learn as much as you can, give yourself every advantage you can by preparing and eliminating distractions—and have fun! Don't spend your whole freshman year beating yourself up and complaining about a lack of playing time! Remember, it's not about how fast you become a starter, it's what you accomplish over your career that matters most! Give yourself time to develop and adjust to the college game! In terms of playing time, coaches would rather get it one week late than one week early and may hold off playing you until they are sure you are ready for it.

#9- GET TO KNOW ATHLETES PLAYING OTHER SPORTS AND REGULAR STUDENTS IN YOUR CLASSES AND DORM. Support the other sports, show up at games and cheer on your classmates who are competing in home matches. Get to know the regular students in your dorm and classes, it's good to have a well-rounded college experience and that includes having different circles of friends outside of your teammates.

#10- STAY ON CAMPUS during the weekends and off days, especially during the first month of college. Life-long friendships are built at college and many of those are formed the first few weeks or months of school. Don't leave at every opportunity to go home and visit friends and family, even if you feel homesick and unattached to your new home. It takes time to build friendships, and it's best to be around those first few weeks while everyone is getting to know each other! Most other students are coming to campus with few or no friends too, you won't be the only one who doesn't know anyone yet.

#11- THE DINING HALL and its all-you-can-eat buffets can help or hurt your nutrition! Stay away from fried foods, pizza, processed meats, soda, sugar drinks, desserts, sugar cereals and try to eat more lean meats, veggies, salads and fruit. Although it's all-you-can-eat, if you are on a calorie-restricted diet, make sure to keep your meals in moderation. If you have a team nutritionist, talk to them about what are some good food choices to make and what serving sizes are healthy for you. Make sure to drink plenty of water, sports drinks and juice between practices and throughout the day to stay hydrated for practice.

#12- **IF YOU ARE ON A CALORIE-RESTRICTED DIET**, make sure to avoid late night fast food meals that tempt every college student. Fried foods, pizza and late night snacks are all-too-available and can easily pack on the pounds!

#13- **SURROUND YOURSELF WITH POSITIVE TEAMMATES.** As a freshman with few friends, choose your circle carefully. You don't want a negative roommate/teammate to get you involved in activities you wouldn't normally get involved in, and you don't want to be surrounded by negative energy. Players who complain, make excuses and whine with every step have a tendency to drag down other teammates with them, and your coaches will pick up quickly which players are approaching the experience with a positive attitude and who is constantly being negative. Keep your distance and find more positive and happy teammates to hang around with.

#14- **CAMPUS POLICE** and your coaches are going to be watching freshman closely, in terms of underage drinking. Several students are normally arrested or cited during the first few weeks at school for underage drinking, DUIs or public intoxication. Understand that the police are LOOKING extra hard those first few weeks of school for underage drinkers! You don't want to start off on the wrong foot with your coaches and the Athletic Department, they have established relationships with the campus and city police so your coaches will be alerted of any problems immediately. Along with fights, non-athletic injuries, misunderstandings and hangovers, alcohol is a major reason freshmen face discipline during their first semester at college.

FRUSTRATION MAKES YOU WANT TO QUIT. THE KEY IS TO PUSH PAST THAT LAYER AND WANT TO DO BETTER NEXT TIME!

ACTION STEPS: REMAIN IN CONTROL

- YOU ARE IN CONTROL OF YOUR DESTINY: EVEN WHEN YOU FEEL HOPELESS AND THAT THE PROCESS WON'T WORK OUT FOR YOU, ALWAYS REMEMBER THAT THERE IS ALWAYS SOMETHING YOU CAN IMPROVE ON, SOME WAY YOU CAN WORK HARDER. THERE ARE ALWAYS MORE COACHES YOU CAN REACH OUT TO, MORE PROGRAMS THAT YOU CAN TRY TO GET EVALUATED BY.

NEXT STEPS – WHAT CAN I DO, OR DO MORE OF, TO CONTINUE TO GET MY NAME OUT THERE:

_____
_____
_____
_____

GOOD LUCK ON YOUR JOURNEY!

KEEP US POSTED WHEN YOU SIGN YOUR SCHOLARSHIP PAPERWORK! EMAIL US AT INFO@001RECRUITTIPS.COM OR TAG PICTURES @001RECRUITTIPS ON TWITTER AND INSTAGRAM!

PLEASE TAKE A MOMENT TO REVIEW THIS BOOK ON <u>AMAZON</u>, TO HELP OTHER STUDENT-ATHLETES AND THEIR FAMILIES FIND SUCCESS IN THE PROCESS!

ABOUT THE AUTHOR

A.P. Bah Bioh has over 16 seasons of experience in collegiate and professional athletics, having been on recruiting staffs at Elon University, UNC-Chapel Hill, the University of Florida and the University of Miami. During that time, Bah Bioh worked primarily with football and men's basketball, but also spent time working with Olympic Sport coaching staffs including softball, women's lacrosse, fencing, golf, tennis and rowing and also spent two seasons with the Cleveland Indians affiliate Burlington Indians as the Clubhouse Manager.

Learning from some of the best mentors in sports, Bah Bioh has worked for three "National Coach of the Year" winners including Urban Meyer (Ohio State Football), Frank Haith (Tulsa Men's Basketball) and Jim Larranaga (Miami Men's Basketball) as well as numerous current NCAA DI head coaches including Steve Addazio (Boston College Football), Larry Fedora (UNC Football), Joel Furtek (Canisius Rowing), Sarah Haney (UNC Women's Rowing), Doc Holliday (Marshall Football), Michael Huger (Bowling Green Men's Basketball), Eric Konkol (Louisiana Tech Men's Basketball), Jenny Levy (UNC Women's Lacrosse), Ron Miller (UNC Fencing), Dan Mullen (Mississippi State Football), Donna Papa (UNC Softball), Sam Paul (UNC Men's Tennis), Beverly Smith (South Carolina Softball), Mark Speir (Western Carolina Football), Charlie Strong (Texas Football), as well as numerous coordinators, assistant coaches and recruiting personnel.

Bah Bioh has been part of numerous championships including the 2007 Florida Gator BCS National Championship; 2006 Florida Gator SEC Football Championship; the 2013 ACC Men's Basketball Championship and Sweet 16 NCAA Tourney run with the Miami Hurricanes that included both tournament and regular-season ACC titles; a 2002 UNC ACC Women's Lacrosse Championship and Final Four finish; a 2001 UNC ACC Softball championship and as a senior, was a 4-year letterwinner with the 1999 Elon Football team that finished with a 9-2 record, one of the best seasons in program history.

Over the years, Bah Bioh has worked with over 30 first-round draft selections (NFL, NBA, MLB) and numerous players who went on to sign professional contracts including Tim Tebow, Cam Newton, Rex Grossman, Shane Larkin, Mike and Maurkice Pouncey, Joe Haden and numerous others.

Bah Bioh has four books available: NCAA Recruit Tips; 100 Most-Asked Recruiting Questions, Answered!; 2017 Edition: NCAA Recruit Tips, 7 Steps to a Scholarship Guide and College Coaches Edition: Recruiting Made Simple.

MORE TIPS - STAY UPDATED!

Sign up for a premium online subscription for just $7.98/month, with no monthly commitment at www.1001RecruitTips.com to help guide you through the process!

Made in the USA
Columbia, SC
23 September 2017